WHIXTIER

SPORTS ENCYCLOPEDIAS FOR KIDS

THE NFL
ENCYCLOPEDIA FOR KIDS

BY BRENDAN FLYNN

Abdo Reference

An Imprint of Abdo Publishing
abdobooks.com

TABLE OF CONTENTS

THE HISTORY OF THE
NATIONAL FOOTBALL LEAGUE

The NFL is wildly popular, with teams regularly selling out their home games.

The National Football League (NFL) started in 1920 with 14 teams. Since then, it has grown into a multibillion-dollar organization. Today, there are 32 teams. NFL games are played in large stadiums packed with cheering fans. Some of these places are old and filled with meaningful histories. Others are more modern. Millions of fans from around the world watch the sport.

There are no sure things in the NFL. Any team can win any game. This is part of what makes the league so exciting for fans. Yet some teams, led by great coaches and players, show a dominance that lasts for many years. These teams often end up in the playoffs. In the playoffs, every game is a sudden-death step toward the Super Bowl—the biggest US sporting event of the year.

Today, the NFL continues to grow in popularity and excitement. However, that wasn't always the case. In the early 1900s, college football was wildly popular but professional football was an unorganized mess. Professional and semipro teams were scattered across the country. There was no official

In February 2021, quarterback Tom Brady led the Tampa Bay Buccaneers to their second Super Bowl win.

rulebook or standings. Also, there was no way to keep players from changing teams whenever they wanted.

THE EARLY DAYS

The owners of four professional teams got together on August 20, 1920. They wanted to talk about organizing their football games. They named their group the American Professional Football Conference and agreed on a set of rules. About one month later, more teams wanted to join and create a professional football league. The new group changed its name to the American Professional Football Association (APFA). APFA leaders created more rules for the sport. In April 1921, the league crowned the Akron Pros from Ohio as its first champion. From there the APFA added even more teams. It started to expand to bigger cities. On June 24, 1922, the APFA changed its name. It was now the National Football League. The number of teams in the NFL rose and fell as leaders added new teams and closed struggling ones.

The NFL was made up almost entirely of white athletes in those days. There were a few Black players in the 1920s, but soon the owners wrongfully decided not to give any Black players contracts. Two former college stars finally broke that barrier in 1946. The Cleveland Rams wanted to move to Los Angeles, California. They wanted to play their games at the LA Coliseum, which was built with public money. Local officials said the Rams had to integrate their roster. So the team agreed to sign Kenny Washington and Woody Strode. Both of these men had played locally at the University of California,

Kenny Washington, *back row on the left*, and Woody Strode, *front row on the right*, made history when they joined the Rams.

Los Angeles (UCLA). Today, Black athletes make up about 70 percent of NFL teams.

GROWING POPULARITY

Rival leagues have challenged the NFL over the years. Two of the most successful ones ended up changing the face of the NFL. In 1944, a group of businesspeople formed the All-America Football Conference (AAFC). The new league tried to form a friendly relationship with the NFL. It agreed not to sign any NFL contract players. The AAFC had eight teams in its first season in 1946. The Cleveland Browns were led by coach Paul Brown. They won all four AAFC titles before the league shut down after the 1949 season. NFL commissioner Bert Bell

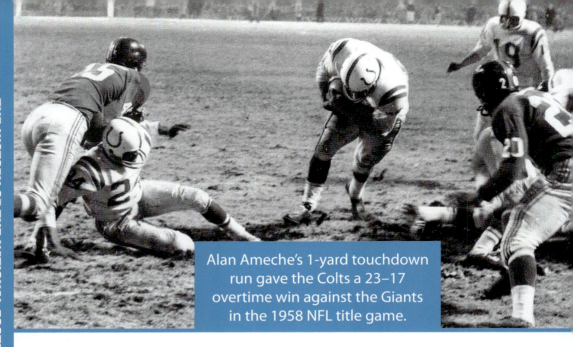

Alan Ameche's 1-yard touchdown run gave the Colts a 23–17 overtime win against the Giants in the 1958 NFL title game.

invited three of the franchises—Cleveland, the San Francisco 49ers, and the Baltimore Colts—to join the NFL.

The popularity of professional football grew in the 1950s as games were shown on television. In 1950, the Rams became the first NFL team to have all their games on television. The 1951 championship between the Rams and Cleveland Browns was the first nationally televised game.

The 1958 NFL Championship Game between the Baltimore Colts and New York Giants pushed professional football's popularity to another level. The nationally broadcast game is still commonly called the "greatest game ever played." It was the first title game to go into overtime. The Colts won in sudden death behind legendary quarterback Johnny Unitas.

BIRTH OF THE AFL

Texas oilman Lamar Hunt tried more than once to buy an NFL team. He was continuously denied. So the young businessman decided to start his own league. He worked with several

The Chargers, *in white*, and Buffalo Bills, *in blue*, were charter members of the AFL in 1960.

other millionaires to create the eight-team American Football League (AFL) in 1959. The new league signed a five-year contract to have games televised by ABC. It started play in September 1960.

The AFL featured a more exciting brand of football. There was more passing and scoring than in the NFL. The AFL added other features still used today. These include player names on jerseys, an official game clock on the scoreboard, and the two-point conversion. The leagues competed for fans and players, but the AFL held its own against the more established NFL. The bidding war for players hit a high point in 1965. Teams from both leagues drafted University of Kansas running back Gale Sayers. He signed with the NFL's Chicago Bears. In addition, both the AFL and NFL wanted to sign University of Alabama quarterback Joe Namath. The AFL offered Namath a massive salary, which he took.

THE MERGER

Leaders from both leagues saw the skyrocketing salaries as a problem. They held secret meetings to discuss combining the leagues. A merger was announced on June 8, 1966. All 24 teams from the two leagues would keep playing. The winners of each league would meet in a championship game after the 1966 season. Starting in 1967, the NFL and AFL would hold one combined draft. This would end the bidding wars that drove up player salaries. In 1970, they would completely merge and the AFL would cease to exist.

The NFL's Green Bay Packers won the first two AFL-NFL World Championship Games, which later became known as

Joe Namath and the New York Jets showed that AFL teams could compete with the NFL.

the Super Bowl. The AFL's New York Jets and Kansas City Chiefs then each claimed a win before the official merger. The combined league's teams were divided into two conferences. The NFL's Cleveland, Pittsburgh, and Baltimore teams joined with the ten AFL teams to form the American Football Conference (AFC). The remaining NFL teams formed the National Football Conference (NFC).

Lamar Hunt, *right*, shares a laugh with NFL commissioner Pete Rozelle before Super Bowl IV in January 1970.

A NEW DAWN FOR FOOTBALL

The new NFL started strong. The 1972 season gave the league one of its most iconic teams. The Miami Dolphins won all 14 of their regular-season games. They continued their winning streak in the playoffs, capping a perfect 17–0 season with a win in Super Bowl VII. Through 2020, it remained the only perfect season in the Super Bowl era.

The NFL's modern era saw a growth in the number of teams. By 1976, the league had grown to 28 teams. Additional expansion in the 1990s and early 2000s resulted in the current

Coach Don Shula gets a ride off the field after the Dolphins completed their perfect 1972 season.

32-team league. Now each conference has 16 teams divided into four divisions of four teams each.

This era also included efforts to increase the sport's popularity outside the United States. Some preseason games were held in Japan, Mexico, England, Canada, Germany, Spain, Ireland, and Australia. Eventually, the league began playing regular-season games abroad as well.

New team owners pay enormous fees to join the league. However, the NFL makes most of its money from deals with television networks that want to show the games. Pete Rozelle became the NFL commissioner in 1960. He understood how important television would be to the success of the league. In 1977, he signed deals with three major television networks. Over the years, these deals became very profitable for the league. The NFL made more than $8 billion on television deals, merchandising, and licensing in 2015. The profits are shared

MONDAY NIGHT FOOTBALL

NFL commissioner Pete Rozelle convinced ABC to make a three-year deal to show weekly Monday night games after the merger. The broadcast was called *Monday Night Football*. The broadcast team included well-known announcer Keith Jackson, commentator Howard Cosell, and former Cowboys quarterback Don Meredith. The announcers were sometimes more entertaining than the game. ABC also showed weekly highlights during halftime. This was a novelty in an age before ESPN and NFL Network showed highlights every day.

A record crowd filled Cleveland Stadium and a large national television audience watched the first Monday night game on September 21, 1970. The Browns beat the visiting New York Jets 31–21. *Monday Night Football* has been part of the NFL's schedule ever since.

Commissioner Pete Rozelle has been credited with helping turn the NFL into America's most popular professional sports league.

among the 32 teams. The league also agreed that games could be streamed on digital platforms such as Amazon and Yahoo. This allows more fans to watch games on their cell phones, tablets, or other devices.

The NFL had several labor disputes over pay, pension benefits, and free agency during Rozelle's term as commissioner. A strike in 1982 shortened the season to nine games. The strike ended with little change in the agreement between players and team owners. Players went on strike again in 1987. This time, owners hired replacement players and continued the season. The strike lasted 24 days and ended without a new agreement.

That strike was followed by a string of lawsuits over the next ten years. These cases continued to fight the NFL's limited free agency. The courts struck down the limited free agency plans in 1991 and 1992. Player Reggie White, along with other athletes,

SUPER BOWL NUMBERING

Kansas City owner Lamar Hunt is credited for using Roman numerals to title each Super Bowl, rather than using normal numbers. He thought Roman numerals would give the game a sense of importance. The league wanted to use numbers to track the Super Bowls rather than naming the games by year. That's because the game was played in a different year than the season it capped. For example, the Super Bowl to decide the winner of the 2018 season was held in February 2019.

The exception to the naming convention was Super Bowl 50. The Roman numeral for 50 is L. However, the NFL didn't like the look of "Super Bowl L." It instead used the number 50. It switched back to Roman numerals a year later.

Los Angeles Raiders players, including Howie Long, actively participated in the 1987 strike.

17

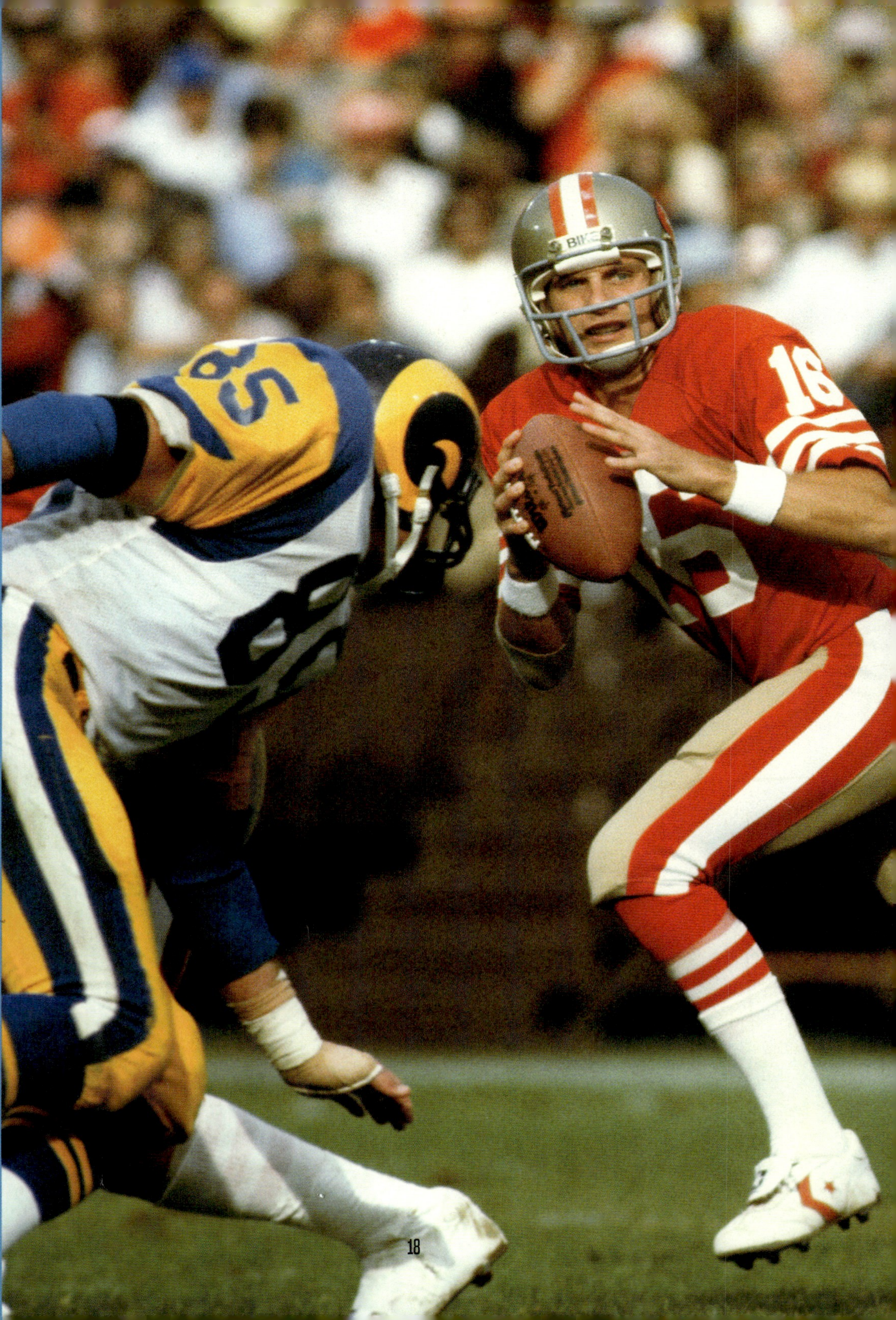

San Francisco 49ers quarterback Joe Montana joined the Hall of Fame in 2000.

filed a class-action suit in 1992. It led to new negotiations and a collective bargaining agreement that included a salary cap and more open free agency.

Despite its occasional off-the-field issues, the NFL is one of the most popular sports leagues in the United States. For example, 26 million people watched the 2021 season kickoff game between the Dallas Cowboys and Tampa Bay Buccaneers. Even in the off-season, fans tune in for events like the NFL Draft and the annual Hall of Fame enshrinement. Fantasy football allows fans of all ages to participate in the games in a different way. All of this has helped make the league a multibillion-dollar industry.

ARIZONA CARDINALS

Wide receiver DeAndre Hopkins looks for an opening during a 2021 game against the Los Angeles Rams.

TEAM HISTORY

The Cardinals trace their roots back to 1920. At first, they were known as the Chicago Cardinals. However, the team got sick of competing with the Chicago Bears. So the team's owners moved the Cardinals to St. Louis, Missouri, in 1960. The team had some tough years. The Cardinals made just three playoff appearances in 28 seasons in St. Louis. They moved to Arizona in 1988. There they battled the desert heat as well as their opponents. The Cardinals got a new domed stadium in 2006. Two years later, the team appeared in its first Super Bowl.

GREATEST PLAYERS

- **Dan Dierdorf**, OT (1971–83)
- **Larry Fitzgerald**, WR (2004–20)
- **Jim Hart**, QB (1966–83)
- **Dick "Night Train" Lane**, CB (1954–59)
- **Patrick Peterson**, CB (2011–20)
- **Luis Sharpe**, T (1982–94)
- **Jackie Smith**, TE (1963–77)
- **Charley Trippi**, RB-QB (1947–55)
- **Kurt Warner**, QB (2005–09)
- **Roger Wehrli**, CB (1969–82)
- **Aeneas Williams**, CB (1991–2000)
- **Larry Wilson**, S (1960–72)

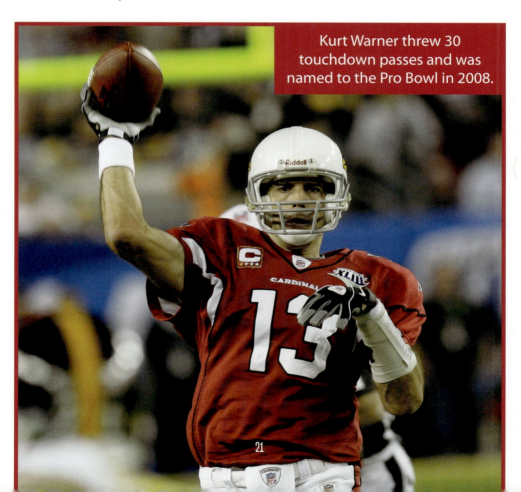

Kurt Warner threw 30 touchdown passes and was named to the Pro Bowl in 2008.

21

TEAM STATS AND RECORDS*

ALL-TIME RECORD

- **Regular Season:** 566–771–41
- **Postseason:** 7–9
- **Super Bowl Record:** 0–1

TOP COACHES

- **Ken Whisenhunt** (2007–12); 45–51 (regular season); 4–2 (postseason)
- **Bruce Arians** (2013–17); 49–30–1 (regular season); 1–2 (postseason)

CAREER OFFENSIVE LEADERS

- **Games played:** Larry Fitzgerald, 263
- **Passing yards:** Jim Hart, 34,639
- **Passing TDs:** Jim Hart, 209
- **Rushing yards:** Ottis Anderson, 7,999
- **Rushing TDs:** Ottis Anderson, 46
- **Receiving yards:** Larry Fitzgerald, 17,492
- **Receiving TDs:** Larry Fitzgerald, 121

CAREER DEFENSIVE LEADERS

- **Games played:** Roger Wehrli, 193
- **Sacks:** Freddie Joe Nunn, 66.5
- **Tackles:** Eric Hill, 785
- **Interceptions:** Larry Wilson, 52
- **Fumble recoveries:** Roger Wehrli, 22

CAREER SPECIAL TEAMS LEADERS

- **Yards per punt:** Andy Lee, 47.3
- **Field goals:** Jim Bakken, 282
- **Field goal percentage:** Jay Feely, 85.2

* All statistics and records in this book are through 2020

Ottis Anderson rushed for 1,000 yards in five of his first six seasons for the Cardinals.

GREATEST SEASONS

In the 2008 season, with quarterback Kurt Warner and wide receivers Anquan Boldin and Larry Fitzgerald, the Cardinals assembled the NFL's second-ranked passing attack. They won the NFC West with a 9–7 record. Then they defeated the Falcons at home in a wild-card game. The next week, the Cardinals traveled to North Carolina. They shocked the Panthers 33–13. That set up a battle with the Eagles back in Arizona. A trip to the Super Bowl was on the line. With less than three minutes to play, Warner hit running back Tim Hightower with an 8-yard touchdown pass. The Cardinals won 32–25. In a thrilling Super Bowl against Pittsburgh, the Cards scored 16 straight points in the fourth quarter to take a 23–20 lead. But the Steelers put together a last-minute drive and scored a touchdown with 35 seconds to play, ending Arizona's Super Bowl dreams.

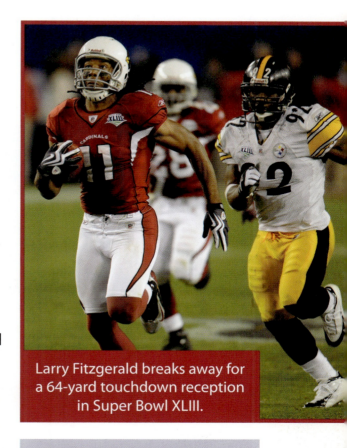

Larry Fitzgerald breaks away for a 64-yard touchdown reception in Super Bowl XLIII.

THE CARDINALS IN MEXICO

The Cardinals and San Francisco 49ers made history in 2005. They were the first NFL teams to play a regular-season game outside the United States. It took place in Mexico City. More than 103,000 fans were there. It was the largest crowd to witness an NFL regular-season game. To make matters sweeter for the Cardinals, they won 31–14.

ATLANTA FALCONS

TEAM HISTORY

College football has always been huge in the South. However, the NFL didn't have a team south of Washington, DC, until the Atlanta Falcons joined in 1966. The team struggled to find its footing. It won just two division titles in its first 32 seasons. But a surprise run to the Super Bowl in 1998 set the stage for future playoff success. Quarterback Matt Ryan put up big numbers after joining the team in 2008. However, through the 2020 season he hadn't been able to win the big one for the Falcons yet.

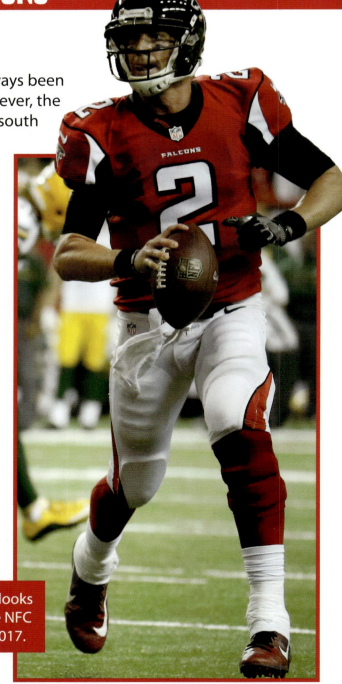

Quarterback Matt Ryan looks for a receiver during the NFC title game in January 2017.

GREATEST PLAYERS

- **Jamal Anderson**, RB (1994–2001)
- **Steve Bartkowski**, QB (1975–85)
- **Claude Humphrey**, DE (1968–74, 1976–78)
- **Julio Jones**, WR (2011–20)
- **Mike Kenn**, T (1978–94)
- **Terance Mathis**, WR (1994–2001)

- **Tommy Nobis**, LB (1966–76)
- **Matt Ryan**, QB (2008–)
- **Gerald Riggs**, RB (1982–88)
- **Deion Sanders**, CB-KR (1989–93)
- **Jessie Tuggle**, LB (1987–2000)
- **Jeff Van Note**, C (1969–86)
- **Michael Vick**, QB (2001–06)

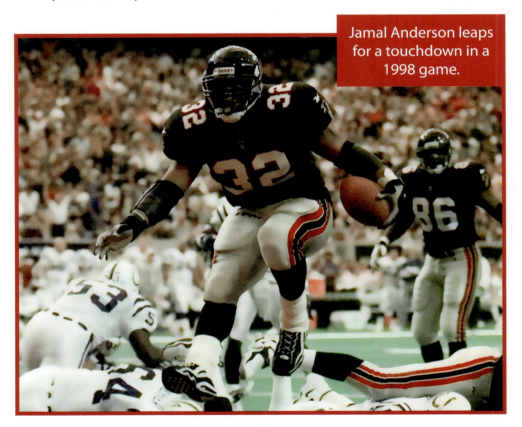

Jamal Anderson leaps for a touchdown in a 1998 game.

TEAM STATS AND RECORDS

ALL-TIME RECORD

- **Regular Season**: 369–473–6
- **Postseason**: 10–14
- **Super Bowl Record**: 0–2

TOP COACHES

- **Dan Reeves** (1997–2003); 49–59–1 (regular season); 3–2 (postseason)
- **Mike Smith** (2008–14); 66–46 (regular season); 1–4 (postseason)

CAREER OFFENSIVE LEADERS

- **Games played**: Mike Kenn, 251
- **Passing yards**: Matt Ryan, 55,767
- **Passing TDs**: Matt Ryan, 347
- **Rushing yards**: Gerald Riggs, 6,631
- **Rushing TDs**: Michael Turner, 60
- **Receiving yards**: Julio Jones, 12,896
- **Receiving TDs**: Roddy White, 63

CAREER DEFENSIVE LEADERS

- **Games played**: Jessie Tuggle, 209
- **Sacks**: John Abraham, 68.5
- **Tackles**: Jessie Tuggle, 1,639
- **Interceptions**: Rolland Lawrence, 39
- **Fumble recoveries**: Greg Brezina, 14

CAREER SPECIAL TEAMS LEADERS

- **Yards per punt**: Matt Bosher, 45.7
- **Field goals**: Matt Bryant, 259
- **Field goal percentage**: Matt Bryant, 87.5

GREATEST SEASONS

The 2016 Falcons had the highest-scoring team in the NFL. Ryan threw 38 touchdown passes. Running back Devonta Freeman rushed for 1,079 yards. Wide receiver Julio Jones posted 1,409 receiving yards. The team went 11–5. It clinched the No. 2 seed in the NFC playoffs. After a divisional-round win over Seattle, the Falcons caught a break when Green Bay beat Dallas, the NFC's top seed. That meant the Falcons got to host the NFC title game. They scored the first 31 points and crushed the Packers 44–21. They took another big lead against the New England Patriots in the Super Bowl, but this time it slipped away. The Patriots trailed 28–3 in the third quarter before rallying to win the game in overtime, denying the Falcons their first NFL title.

Julio Jones played a key role in helping the 2016 Falcons reach the Super Bowl.

BUILDING A NEW STADIUM

The Falcons left the Georgia Dome after the 2016 season. But they didn't move far. Their new home was built right next door. Mercedes-Benz Stadium opened in 2017. Unlike the Georgia Dome, the roof on the new stadium opens. But it can stay closed in case of rain or extreme heat. The stadium holds 71,000 fans.

BALTIMORE RAVENS

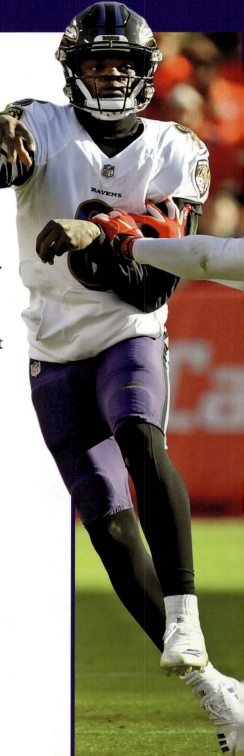

TEAM HISTORY

The Baltimore Ravens didn't join the NFL until 1996. Cleveland Browns owner Art Modell fought for years to get a new stadium for his team. Finally he gave up and moved them to Baltimore, Maryland. That city had lost its own team, the Colts, in 1984. While in Cleveland, the Browns had never reached the Super Bowl. But once in Baltimore, the newly named Ravens took only five seasons to build an NFL championship team. Since then, the Ravens have been one of the league's most consistent winners. They often have a strong defense and running game.

GREATEST PLAYERS

- **Peter Boulware**, LB (1997–2005)
- **Joe Flacco**, QB (2008–18)
- **Lamar Jackson**, QB (2018–)
- **Jamal Lewis**, RB (2000, 2002–06)
- **Ray Lewis**, LB (1996–12)
- **Chris McAlister**, CB (1999–2008)
- **C. J. Mosley**, LB (2014–18)
- **Jonathan Ogden**, OT (1996–2007)
- **Ed Reed**, S (2002–12)
- **Matt Stover**, K (1996–2008)
- **Terrell Suggs**, LB (2003–18)
- **Rod Woodson**, DB (1998–2001)

Quarterback Lamar Jackson throws on the run in a 2018 game against the Kansas City Chiefs.

TEAM STATS AND RECORDS

ALL-TIME RECORD
- **Regular Season**: 225–174–1
- **Postseason**: 16–11
- **Super Bowl Record**: 2–0

TOP COACHES
- **Brian Billick** (1999–2007); 80–64 (regular season); 5–3, 1 Super Bowl title (postseason)
- **John Harbaugh** (2008–); 129–79 (regular season); 11–8, 1 Super Bowl title (postseason)

CAREER OFFENSIVE LEADERS
- **Games played**: Jonathan Ogden and Marshal Yanda, 177
- **Passing yards**: Joe Flacco, 38,245
- **Passing TDs**: Joe Flacco, 212
- **Rushing yards**: Jamal Lewis, 7,801
- **Rushing TDs**: Jamal Lewis, 45
- **Receiving yards**: Derrick Mason, 5,777
- **Receiving TDs**: Todd Heap, 41

CAREER DEFENSIVE LEADERS
- **Games played**: Terrell Suggs, 229
- **Sacks**: Terrell Suggs, 132.5
- **Tackles**: Ray Lewis, 1,568
- **Interceptions**: Ed Reed, 61
- **Fumble recoveries**: Ray Lewis, 20

CAREER SPECIAL TEAMS LEADERS
- **Yards per punt**: Sam Koch, 45.3
- **Field goals**: Matt Stover, 354
- **Field goal percentage**: Justin Tucker, 90.7

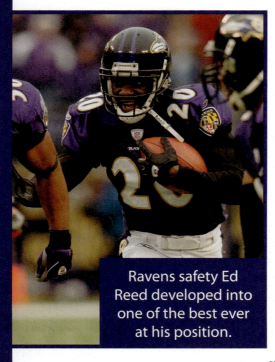

Ravens safety Ed Reed developed into one of the best ever at his position.

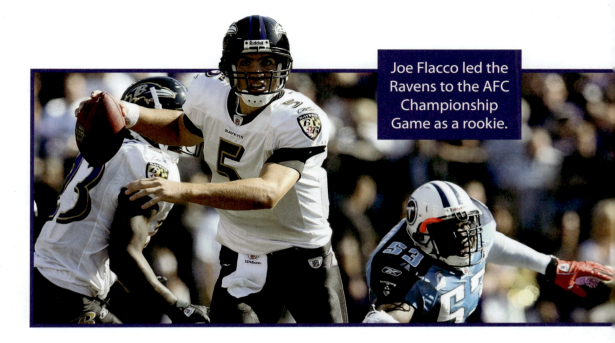

Joe Flacco led the Ravens to the AFC Championship Game as a rookie.

GREATEST SEASONS

The 2000 Ravens had what many believe to be the greatest defense in NFL history. It was led by Hall of Fame linebacker Ray Lewis. The Ravens held their opponents to just over ten points per game. Quarterback Trent Dilfer and the offense weren't as dominant, but they scored enough to win 12 games that season. In the playoffs, the defense got even tougher. In four postseason games, the Ravens defense gave up just one touchdown. Baltimore rolled through the AFC playoffs. Then they stopped the New York Giants in the Super Bowl, forcing five turnovers in a 34–7 victory.

ED REED'S TOUCHDOWNS

Ravens Hall of Fame safety Ed Reed was also a standout on special teams. He became the first player in NFL history to score a touchdown on an interception return, a blocked punt, a punt return, and a fumble return. He scored 13 touchdowns in his career. He recorded seven touchdowns on interceptions, three on blocked punts, two on fumble returns, and one on a punt return.

Quarterback Josh Allen looks for an open receiver during a 2018 game.

TEAM HISTORY

Owner Ralph Wilson brought the Buffalo Bills into the AFL in 1960. In their fourth season, the Bills won the first of four straight division titles. Two of those seasons—1964 and 1965—ended with the Bills as AFL champions. After making the playoffs just three times over the next 21 seasons, the Bills launched another era of excellence. They won more games in the 1990s than any other AFC team.

GREATEST PLAYERS

- **Josh Allen**, QB (2018–)
- **Joe DeLamielleure**, G (1973–79, 1985)
- **Joe Ferguson**, QB (1973–84)
- **Jim Kelly**, QB (1986–96)
- **Jack Kemp**, QB (1962–69)
- **Reggie McKenzie**, G (1972–82)
- **Eric Moulds**, WR (1996–2005)
- **Andre Reed**, WR (1985–99)
- **Billy Shaw**, G (1961–69)
- **O. J. Simpson**, RB (1969–77)
- **Bruce Smith**, DE (1985–99)
- **Thurman Thomas**, RB (1988–99)

FROM FOOTBALL TO POLITICS

Jack Kemp was the quarterback of the Bills' 1964 and 1965 AFL championship teams. He went on to a successful career in politics. He served nine terms in the US House of Representatives representing western New York. He also served as the secretary of Housing and Urban Development. He was the Republican Party's nominee for vice president in 1996. Kemp died in 2009 at age 73.

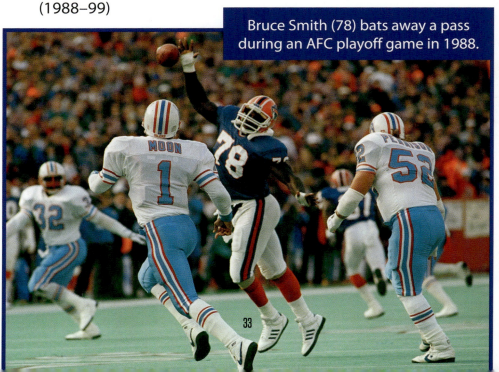

Bruce Smith (78) bats away a pass during an AFC playoff game in 1988.

TEAM STATS AND RECORDS

ALL-TIME RECORD

- **Regular Season**: 438–486–8
- **Postseason**: 16–18
- **Super Bowl Record**: 0–4

TOP COACHES

- **Lou Saban** (1962–65, 1972–76); 68–45–4 (regular season); 2–2 (postseason)
- **Marv Levy** (1986–97); 112–70 (regular season); 11–8 (postseason)

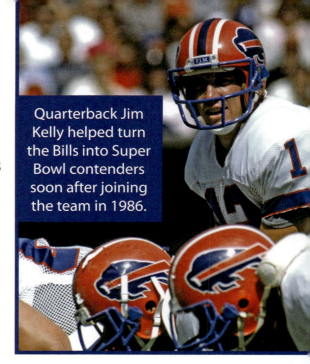

Quarterback Jim Kelly helped turn the Bills into Super Bowl contenders soon after joining the team in 1986.

CAREER OFFENSIVE LEADERS

- **Games played**: Andre Reed, 221
- **Passing yards**: Jim Kelly, 35,467
- **Passing TDs**: Jim Kelly, 237
- **Rushing yards**: Thurman Thomas, 11,938
- **Rushing TDs**: Thurman Thomas, 65
- **Receiving yards**: Andre Reed, 13,095
- **Receiving TDs**: Andre Reed, 86

CAREER DEFENSIVE LEADERS

- **Games played**: Bruce Smith, 217
- **Sacks**: Bruce Smith, 171
- **Tackles**: Darryl Talley, 1,095
- **Interceptions**: Butch Byrd, 40
- **Fumble recoveries**: Cornelius Bennett, 19

CAREER SPECIAL TEAMS LEADERS

- **Yards per punt**: Corey Bojorquez, 45.0
- **Field goals**: Steve Christie, 234
- **Field goal percentage**: Dan Carpenter, 86.5

GREATEST SEASONS

Led by a trio of future Hall of Famers—quarterback Jim Kelly, running back Thurman Thomas, and wide receiver Andre Reed—the Bills had one of the top offensive machines in NFL history. Between 1988 and 1996, Buffalo won six division titles. They also made two other playoff appearances over a nine-year run. The Bills became the first—and through 2020, only—team to reach four straight Super Bowls. Unfortunately, they lost all four. This was the only blemish on an otherwise dominant era.

Running back Thurman Thomas was a threat in all weather.

CAROLINA PANTHERS

TEAM HISTORY

The Carolina Panthers joined the NFL in 1995. They started off strong, going 7–9 in their first season and reaching the NFC Championship Game in their second season. In 2003, veteran quarterback Jake Delhomme led them to a surprising Super Bowl appearance, where they lost to the New England Patriots on a last-second field goal. Carolina made it back to the NFC title game in 2005. However, the Panthers suffered through some lean years before returning to the Super Bowl in 2015.

GREATEST PLAYERS

- **Thomas Davis**, LB (2005–18)
- **Jake Delhomme**, QB (2003–09)
- **Luke Kuechly**, LB (2012–19)
- **Christian McCaffrey**, RB (2017–)
- **Sam Mills**, LB (1995–97)
- **Muhsin Muhammad**, WR (1996–2004, 2008–09)
- **Cam Newton**, QB (2011–19)
- **Greg Olsen**, TE (2011–19)
- **Julius Peppers**, DE (2002–09, 2017–18)
- **Steve Smith**, WR (2001–13)
- **Jonathan Stewart**, RB (2008–17)
- **DeAngelo Williams**, RB (2006–14)

ONE TEAM, TWO STATES

The Panthers are unusual among US sports teams. They are referred to by a region, not a city or state. That is because the Panthers represent both North Carolina and South Carolina. When the Panthers made their run to Super Bowl 50, the hashtag #OneCarolina was developed. It symbolized that when it comes to rooting for the Panthers, both Carolinas were in it together.

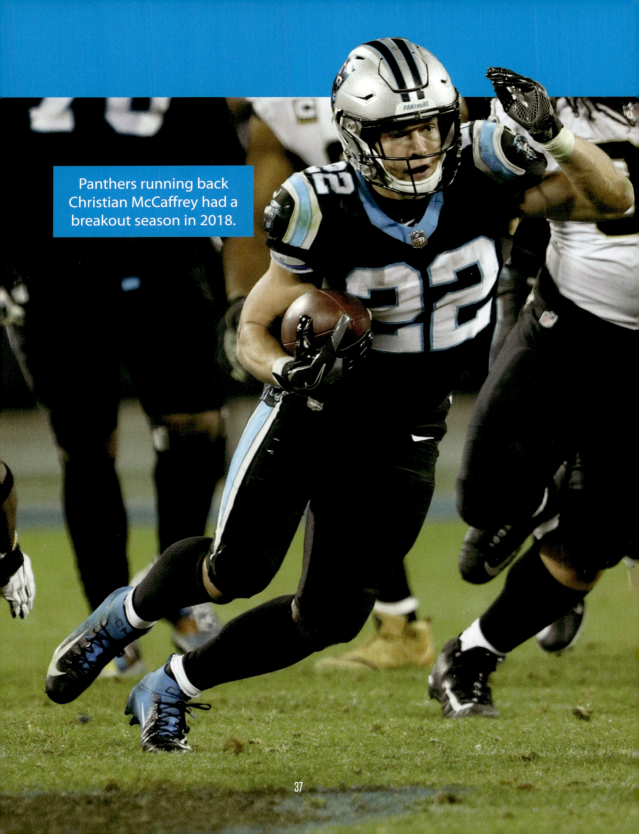

Panthers running back Christian McCaffrey had a breakout season in 2018.

TEAM STATS AND RECORDS

ALL-TIME RECORD

- **Regular Season**: 200–215–1
- **Postseason**: 9–8
- **Super Bowl Record**: 0–2

TOP COACHES

- **John Fox** (2002–10); 73–71 (regular season); 5–3, (postseason)
- **Ron Rivera** (2011–19); 76–63–1 (regular season); 3–4 (postseason)

CAREER OFFENSIVE LEADERS

- **Games played**: Steve Smith, 182
- **Passing yards**: Cam Newton, 29,041
- **Passing TDs**: Cam Newton, 182
- **Rushing yards**: Jonathan Stewart, 7,318
- **Rushing TDs**: Cam Newton, 58
- **Receiving yards**: Steve Smith, 12,197
- **Receiving TDs**: Steve Smith, 67

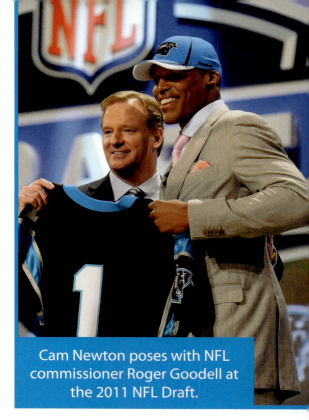

Cam Newton poses with NFL commissioner Roger Goodell at the 2011 NFL Draft.

CAREER DEFENSIVE LEADERS

- **Games played**: Thomas Davis, 176
- **Sacks**: Julius Peppers, 97
- **Tackles**: Thomas Davis, 789
- **Interceptions**: Chris Gamble, 27
- **Fumble recoveries**: Mike Minter and Thomas Davis, 11

CAREER SPECIAL TEAMS LEADERS

- **Yards per punt**: Todd Sauerbrun, 45.5
- **Field goals**: John Kasay, 351
- **Field goal percentage**: Graham Gano, 85.5

GREATEST SEASONS

The 2015 Panthers set a team record by going 15–1. They started the season with 14 straight wins. This set them up to become the third team in the Super Bowl era to have an unbeaten regular season. However, they lost to the Atlanta Falcons in late December. Still, quarterback Cam Newton directed a diverse offensive attack. Linebackers Luke Kuechly and Thomas Davis led a strong defense. Both of these things made the Panthers tough to beat. After home playoff victories over Seattle and Arizona, they faced the Denver Broncos in the Super Bowl. The Broncos' defense proved to be too much for the Panthers. They saw their near-perfect season end with a 24–10 loss.

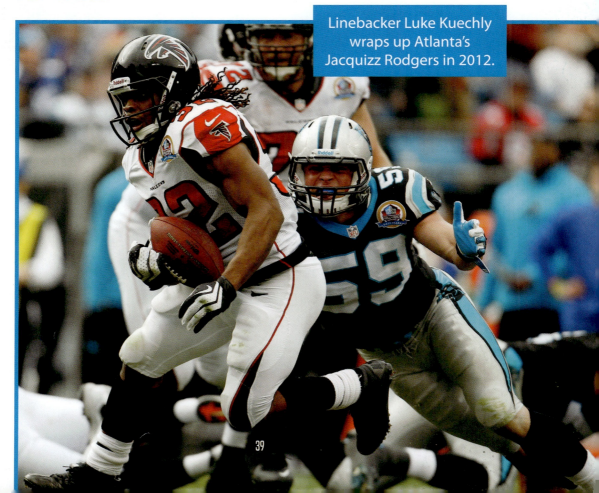

Linebacker Luke Kuechly wraps up Atlanta's Jacquizz Rodgers in 2012.

CHICAGO BEARS

Khalil Mack attempts to stop a Saints wide receiver during a 2021 game.

TEAM HISTORY

The Bears trace their roots back to the 1920 Decatur Staleys of the APFA. In 1922, they became known as the Chicago Bears. Under legendary head coach and team owner George Halas, the team dominated the NFL. It won six league titles and three other division championships between 1932 and 1943. The Bears had another stretch of success in the mid-1980s behind head coach Mike Ditka and a bruising defense.

AN UNUSUAL FIELD

Arena football was still 54 years away when bad weather forced the Bears and Portsmouth Spartans to play the first indoor title game in 1932. The improvised field in Chicago Stadium was sized like arena ball: only 80 yards (73 m) long. Hash marks were first used in this game. Straw and dirt were put over the surface, which had just hosted a circus. The Bears won 9–0.

GREATEST PLAYERS

- **Doug Atkins**, DE (1955–66)
- **Dick Butkus**, LB (1965–73)
- **Jay Cutler**, QB (2009–16)
- **Bill George**, LB (1952–65)
- **Red Grange**, RB (1925, 1929–34)
- **Dan Hampton**, DE (1979–90)
- **Sid Luckman**, QB (1939–50)
- **Bronko Nagurski**, FB-DT (1930–37, 1943)
- **Walter Payton**, RB (1975–87)
- **Gale Sayers**, RB (1965–71)
- **Mike Singletary**, LB (1981–92)
- **Brian Urlacher**, LB (2000–12)

Walter Payton heads downfield with the ball during Super Bowl XX.

TEAM STATS AND RECORDS

ALL-TIME RECORD

- **Regular Season**: 777–599–42
- **Postseason**: 17–20
- **Super Bowl Record**: 1–1

TOP COACHES

- **George Halas** (1920–29, 1933–42, 1946–67); 318–148–31 (regular season); 6–3, 6 NFL titles (postseason)
- **Mike Ditka** (1982–92); 106–62 (regular season); 6–6, 1 Super Bowl title (postseason)

CAREER OFFENSIVE LEADERS

- **Games played**: Olin Kreutz, 191
- **Passing yards**: Jay Cutler, 23,443
- **Passing TDs**: Jay Cutler, 154
- **Rushing yards**: Walter Payton, 16,726
- **Rushing TDs**: Walter Payton, 110
- **Receiving yards**: Johnny Morris, 5,059
- **Receiving TDs**: Ken Kavanaugh, 50

CAREER DEFENSIVE LEADERS

- **Games played**: Steve McMichael, 191
- **Sacks**: Richard Dent, 124.5
- **Tackles**: Brian Urlacher, 1,046
- **Interceptions**: Gary Fencik, 38
- **Fumble recoveries**: Dick Butkus, 27

CAREER SPECIAL TEAMS LEADERS

- **Yards per punt**: Pat O'Donnell, 45.0
- **Field goals**: Robbie Gould, 276
- **Field goal percentage**: Robbie Gould, 85.4

GREATEST SEASONS

Led by Hall of Famers such as running back Walter Payton, defensive ends Richard Dent and Dan Hampton, and linebacker Mike Singletary, the 1985 Bears steamrolled the league. They started the season with 12 straight wins. They had fans talking about an undefeated season. The Bears ended up losing a shootout in Miami in early December, but that just sparked the rest of their amazing run. They finished the season 15–1. They cruised through three postseason opponents by a combined score of 91–10. Their 46–10 thrashing of the New England Patriots gave Chicago its first Super Bowl championship.

From left, Willie Gault, Steve McMichael, coach Mike Ditka, William Perry, and Maury Buford helped the 1985 Bears win the team's lone Super Bowl.

CINCINNATI BENGALS

TEAM HISTORY

The Cincinnati Bengals started playing in 1968. They won two division titles in a six-year span in the early 1970s. After a number of lean years, they won the AFC in 1981. They won it again in 1988, although both years ended with losses to the San Francisco 49ers in the Super Bowl. The Bengals had another run of success after hiring Marvin Lewis as head coach in 2003. But Lewis's teams consistently fell short in the playoffs, leaving the Bengals still searching for their first Super Bowl title.

Quarterback Joe Burrow (9) joined the Bengals in 2020. He was the No. 1 draft pick that year.

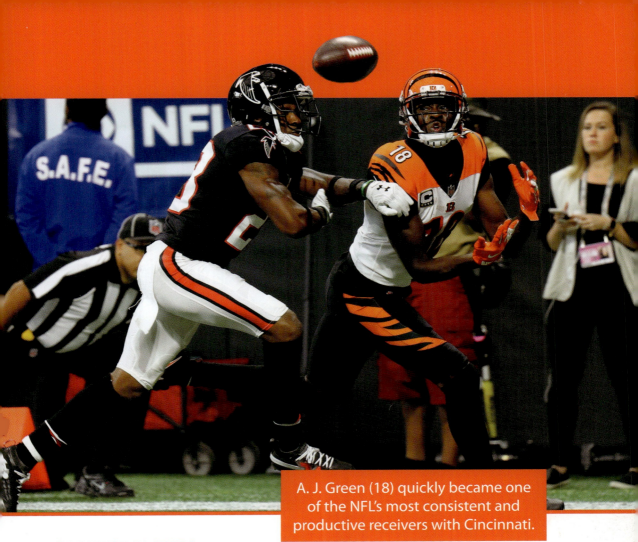

A. J. Green (18) quickly became one of the NFL's most consistent and productive receivers with Cincinnati.

GREATEST PLAYERS

- **Ken Anderson**, QB (1971–86)
- **Geno Atkins**, DT (2010–20)
- **Cris Collinsworth**, WR (1981–88)
- **Isaac Curtis**, WR (1973–84)
- **Andy Dalton**, QB (2011–19)
- **Corey Dillon**, RB (1997–2003)

- **Boomer Esiason**, QB (1984–92, 1997)
- **A. J. Green**, WR (2011–20)
- **Anthony Munoz**, OT (1980–92)
- **Carson Palmer**, QB (2004– 10)
- **Ken Riley**, DB (1969–83)
- **Andrew Whitworth**, T (2006–16)

ALL-TIME RECORD

- **Regular Season**: 363–452–5
- **Postseason**: 5–14
- **Super Bowl Record**: 0–2

TOP COACHES

- **Sam Wyche** (1984–91); 61–66 (regular season); 3–2 (postseason)
- **Marvin Lewis** (2003–18); 131–122–3 (regular season); 0–7 (postseason)

CAREER OFFENSIVE LEADERS

- **Games played**: Ken Anderson, 192
- **Passing yards**: Ken Anderson, 32,838
- **Passing TDs**: Andy Dalton, 204
- **Rushing yards**: Corey Dillon, 8,061
- **Rushing TDs**: Pete Johnson, 64
- **Receiving yards**: Chad Johnson, 10,783
- **Receiving TDs**: Chad Johnson, 66

CAREER DEFENSIVE LEADERS

- **Games played**: Ken Riley, 207
- **Sacks**: Carlos Dunlap, 82.5
- **Tackles**: Tim Krumrie, 1,008
- **Interceptions**: Ken Riley, 65
- **Fumble recoveries**: Reggie Williams, 23

CAREER SPECIAL TEAMS LEADERS

- **Yards per punt**: Kevin Huber, 45.3
- **Field goals**: Jim Breech, 225
- **Field goal percentage**: Shayne Graham, 86.8

COACH LEWIS

Marvin Lewis was the second-longest tenured head coach in the NFL when he moved on from Cincinnati after the 2018 season. Only New England Patriots coach Bill Belichick had been with his team longer than the 16 seasons Lewis spent in Cincinnati. Lewis's 131 career victories made him twenty-ninth on the all-time list.

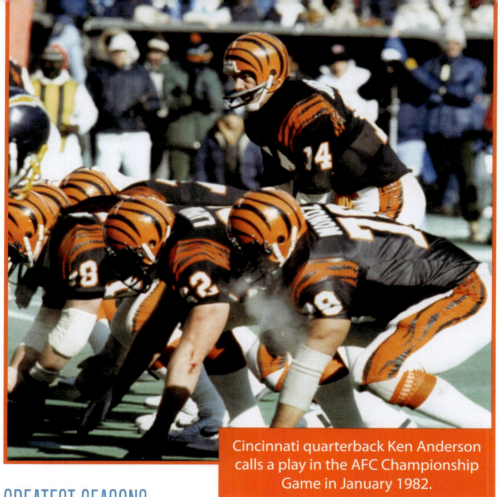

Cincinnati quarterback Ken Anderson calls a play in the AFC Championship Game in January 1982.

GREATEST SEASONS

After three straight last-place finishes, expectations for the Bengals were low going into the 1981 season. But behind quarterback Ken Anderson, fullback Pete Johnson, and rookie wide receiver Cris Collinsworth, the team's offense caught fire. They won seven of their last eight regular-season games to win the AFC Central Division. Their 12–4 record was the best in the conference. This gave them home-field advantage in the playoffs. That proved important as the high-flying San Diego Chargers came to town for the AFC Championship Game. On a cold game day, the Chargers' offense struggled. Anderson threw two touchdown passes, and the Bengals won 27–7 to reach their first Super Bowl. Although they lost that game, the team gave its fans a season to remember.

TEAM HISTORY

The Cleveland Browns began playing in 1946. They spent their first four years in the AAFC, winning the league title each year. After joining the NFL in 1950, they won the title that year too. Cleveland went on to reach the NFL Championship Game for the next five years, winning titles in 1954 and 1955. The great running back Jim Brown helped the team win many games in the late 1950s and early 1960s. Over the years, Cleveland had a number of close calls but never made it to the Super Bowl. After a long battle over a new stadium, the Browns' owner moved the team to Baltimore in 1996. The NFL gave a new team to Cleveland, Ohio, and let it keep the Browns name and records. The new Browns began playing in 1999, but they've struggled to repeat the success of the team's earlier days.

GREATEST PLAYERS

- **Jim Brown**, RB (1957–65)
- **Otto Graham**, QB (1946–55)
- **Lou Groza**, OT-K (1946–59, 1961–67)
- **Leroy Kelly**, RB (1964–73)
- **Bernie Kosar**, QB (1985–93)
- **Dante Lavelli**, WR (1946–56)
- **Clay Matthews**, LB (1978–93)
- **Marion Motley**, RB (1946–53)
- **Ozzie Newsome**, TE (1978–90)
- **Brian Sipe**, QB (1974–83)
- **Joe Thomas**, OT, 2007–17)
- **Paul Warfield**, WR (1964–69, 1976–77)

Cleveland running back Jim Brown looks on during a game in 1965.

48

Baker Mayfield's strong play since arriving in 2018 had Browns fans looking forward to the future.

TEAM STATS AND RECORDS

ALL-TIME RECORD
- **Regular Season:** 533–509–14
- **Postseason:** 17–21
- **Super Bowl Record:** 0–0

TOP COACHES
- **Paul Brown** (1946–62); 158–48–8 (regular season); 9–5, 4 AAFC championships, 3 NFL championships (postseason)
- **Blanton Collier** (1963–70); 76–34–2 (regular season); 3–4, 1 NFL championship (postseason)

CAREER OFFENSIVE LEADERS
- **Games played:** Lou Groza, 268
- **Passing yards:** Brian Sipe, 23,713
- **Passing TDs:** Otto Graham, 174
- **Rushing yards:** Jim Brown, 12,312
- **Rushing TDs:** Jim Brown, 106
- **Receiving yards:** Ozzie Newsome, 7,980
- **Receiving TDs:** Gary Collins, 70

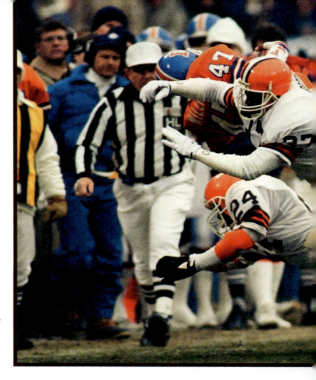

CAREER DEFENSIVE LEADERS
- **Games played:** Clay Matthews, 232
- **Sacks:** Clay Matthews, 62
- **Tackles:** Clay Matthews, 1,430
- **Interceptions:** Thom Darden, 45
- **Fumble recoveries:** Paul Wiggin and Len Ford, 19

CAREER SPECIAL TEAMS LEADERS
- **Yards per punt:** Britton Colquitt, 46.1
- **Field goals:** Phil Dawson, 305
- **Field goal percentage:** Phil Dawson, 84.0

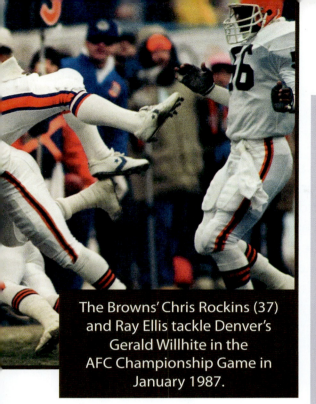

The Browns' Chris Rockins (37) and Ray Ellis tackle Denver's Gerald Willhite in the AFC Championship Game in January 1987.

JIM BROWN

The debate has raged for decades: Who is the best player in NFL history? A small number of stars are generally mentioned. And Pro Football Hall of Fame running back Jim Brown is almost always in the mix.

Brown was drafted by Cleveland in 1957. He dominated the NFL from the start. In 1963, Brown ran for 1,863 yards, an NFL record that stood for years. His single-season average of 6.4 yards per attempt that year was the best in league history for any back with at least 200 carries. Kansas City Chiefs tailback Jamaal Charles matched the record in 2010. Some of Brown's other records have since been broken. It's possible that Brown would still hold many of them had he not retired at age 29 to pursue an acting career.

GREATEST SEASONS

Starting in 1985, the Browns won three straight division titles. Their best team of the three was the 1986 club. It went 12–4 with quarterback Bernie Kosar running the offense and linebacker Clay Matthews leading the defense. The Browns suffered a heartbreaking defeat to the Denver Broncos in overtime in the AFC Championship Game that year. They had a chance for revenge in Denver the next year, but a late fumble kept them from reaching the Super Bowl again.

TEAM HISTORY

The Dallas Cowboys joined the NFL in 1960. They didn't win a game in their first year. But it didn't take long for head coach Tom Landry to turn them into winners. No team won more than the Cowboys in the 1970s. Over the decade, they averaged 10.5 wins per season. They also won five NFC titles and two Super Bowls. The next great era came under head coach Jimmy Johnson in the early 1990s and later coach Barry Switzer. Dallas won three more Super Bowls in a four-year span.

GREATEST PLAYERS

- **Troy Aikman**, QB (1989–2000)
- **Tony Dorsett**, RB (1977–87)
- **Ezekiel Elliott**, RB (2016–)
- **Chuck Howley**, LB (1961–73)
- **Michael Irvin**, WR (1988–99)
- **Bob Lilly**, DT (1961–74)
- **Dak Prescott**, QB (2016–)
- **Tony Romo**, QB (2004–16)
- **Emmitt Smith**, RB (1990–2002)
- **Roger Staubach**, QB (1969–79)
- **Randy White**, DT (1975–88)
- **Jason Witten**, TE (2003–17, 2019)

Ezekiel Elliott dives into the end zone to score his first NFL touchdown.

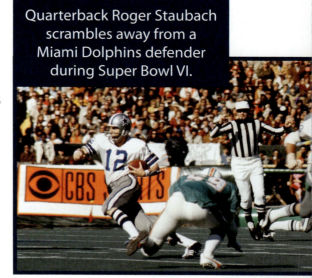

TEAM STATS AND RECORDS

ALL-TIME RECORD
- **Regular Season**: 526–398–6
- **Postseason**: 35–28
- **Super Bowl Record**: 5–3

TOP COACHES
- **Tom Landry** (1960–88); 250–162–6 (regular season); 20–16, 2 Super Bowl titles (postseason)
- **Jimmy Johnson** (1989–93); 44–36 (regular season); 7–1, 2 Super Bowl titles (postseason)
- **Jason Garrett** (2010–19); 85–67 (regular season); 2–3 (postseason)

CAREER OFFENSIVE LEADERS
- **Games played**: Jason Witten, 255
- **Passing yards**: Tony Romo, 34,183
- **Passing TDs**: Tony Romo, 248
- **Rushing yards**: Emmitt Smith, 17,162
- **Rushing TDs**: Emmitt Smith, 153
- **Receiving yards**: Jason Witten, 12,977
- **Receiving TDs**: Dez Bryant, 73

CAREER DEFENSIVE LEADERS
- **Games played**: Ed Jones, 224
- **Sacks**: DeMarcus Ware, 117
- **Tackles**: Darren Woodson, 827
- **Interceptions**: Mel Renfro, 52
- **Fumble recoveries**: Ed Jones, 19

CAREER SPECIAL TEAMS LEADERS
- **Yards per punt**: Mat McBriar, 45.3
- **Field goals**: Dan Bailey, 186
- **Field goal percentage**: Dan Bailey, 88.2

Quarterback Roger Staubach scrambles away from a Miami Dolphins defender during Super Bowl VI.

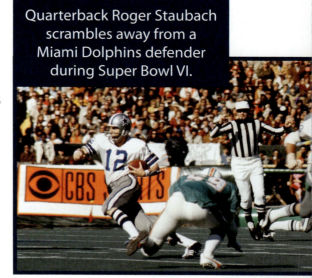

Emmitt Smith helped form the Cowboys' explosive offensive attack during the 1990s.

GREATEST SEASONS

The early 1990s Cowboys teams were led by the "Triplets." That was the nickname for quarterback Troy Aikman, tailback Emmitt Smith, and wide receiver Michael Irvin. All were future Hall of Famers, as was guard Larry Allen. Hall of Fame defensive end Charles Haley and cornerback Deion Sanders also starred for those Cowboy teams. From 1992 to 1995, Dallas went 49–15 in the regular season. They won three Super Bowls by an average of almost 21 points.

COACH LANDRY

As Dallas's head coach, Tom Landry helped develop the 4–3 defense. That scheme used four down linemen and three linebackers. Many teams still use that formation today. Landry also introduced offensive motion. He popularized the shotgun formation, used situational substitutions, and created the flex defense. In 2020, Landry stood fourth on the all-time list for coaching victories.

DENVER BRONCOS

TEAM HISTORY

The Broncos have been in Denver since 1960. They were one of eight teams in the AFL's first season. They didn't have much early success, failing to reach the playoffs until 1977. But they made the Super Bowl that year behind their Orange Crush defense. Since then, the Broncos have been regulars in the AFC playoffs. They have won Super Bowls with two of the greatest quarterbacks in NFL history at the helm: John Elway and Peyton Manning.

GREATEST PLAYERS

- **Steve Atwater**, S (1989–98)
- **Champ Bailey**, CB (2004–13)
- **Terrell Davis**, RB (1995–2001)
- **John Elway**, QB (1983–98)
- **Randy Gradishar**, LB (1974–83)
- **Tom Jackson**, LB (1973–86)
- **Floyd Little**, RB (1967–75)
- **Karl Mecklenburg**, LB (1983–94)
- **Von Miller**, LB (2011–19)
- **Shannon Sharpe**, TE (1990–99, 2002–03)
- **Dennis Smith**, S (1981–94)
- **Rod Smith**, WR (1995–2006)

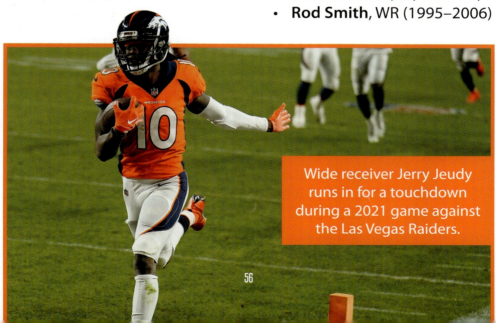

Wide receiver Jerry Jeudy runs in for a touchdown during a 2021 game against the Las Vegas Raiders.

Lyle Alzado (77), Bob Swenson (51), and Randy Gradishar (53) were part of the Orange Crush defense in the 1970s.

TEAM STATS AND RECORDS

ALL-TIME RECORD

- **Regular Season**: 488–434–10
- **Postseason**: 23–19
- **Super Bowl Record**: 3–5

TOP COACHES

- **Dan Reeves** (1981–92); 110–73–1 (regular season); 7–6 (postseason)
- **Mike Shanahan** (1995–2008); 138–86 (regular season); 8–5, 2 Super Bowl titles (postseason)

CAREER OFFENSIVE LEADERS

- **Games played:** John Elway, 234
- **Passing yards:** John Elway, 51,475
- **Passing TDs:** John Elway, 300
- **Rushing yards:** Terrell Davis, 7,607
- **Rushing TDs:** Terrell Davis, 60
- **Receiving yards:** Rod Smith, 11,389
- **Receiving TDs:** Rod Smith, 68

CAREER DEFENSIVE LEADERS

- **Games played:** Tom Jackson, 191
- **Sacks:** Von Miller, 106
- **Tackles:** Dennis Smith, 1,152
- **Interceptions:** Steve Foley, 44
- **Fumble recoveries:** Bill Thompson, 21

CAREER SPECIAL TEAMS LEADERS

- **Yards per punt:** Riley Dixon, 45.7
- **Field goals:** Jason Elam, 395
- **Field goal percentage:** Matt Prater, 82.9

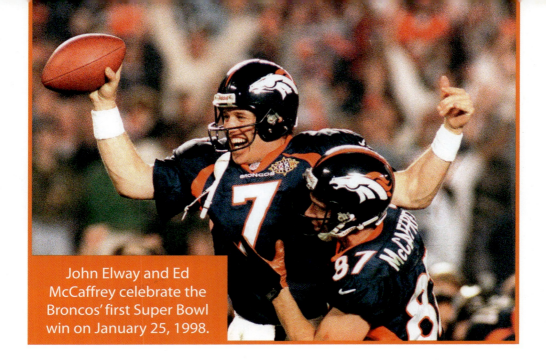

John Elway and Ed McCaffrey celebrate the Broncos' first Super Bowl win on January 25, 1998.

GREATEST SEASONS

Elway led the Broncos to three AFC titles in the late 1980s. However, the team was blown out in the Super Bowl all three years. NFL fans were beginning to wonder if Elway would ever win the big one.

In 1995, the Broncos drafted a running back who could help Elway over the hump. Though Terrell Davis played only four full seasons before injuries took their toll, he made the Pro Football Hall of Fame. Davis rushed for 1,117 yards as a rookie. He improved that total each year. In 1998 he peaked at 2,008 yards and 21 touchdowns. He also won the 1998 NFL's Most Valuable Player (MVP) Award. In addition, he helped Elway win Super Bowls in his final two NFL seasons.

PLAYING WITH ELWAY

Mark Schlereth was a guard for the Broncos. He played with Elway and once said, "You always knew you had a chance with [Elway] on the football field at the end of the game. You felt so confident running up to the line of scrimmage. You'd be excited just to see what he'd do this time. And you could see the looks of fear in the eyes of guys across the line."

DETROIT LIONS

Defensive end Romeo Okwara faces off with a Vikings player in a January 2021 game in Detroit.

TEAM HISTORY

The Lions trace their roots back to the Portsmouth Spartans, who joined the NFL in 1930. After four years in Ohio, they moved north to Detroit, Michigan. They changed their name to the Lions. The team won its first NFL title in 1935. After a long stretch of mediocre teams, in the 1950s the Lions built a winner behind quarterback

THANKSGIVING DAY FOOTBALL

The Lions scheduled a home game on Thanksgiving Day in 1934. They lost to the Chicago Bears 19–16. But the Lions continued playing the Bears on Thanksgiving through 1938. Detroit stopped the Turkey Day tradition for a while. But they picked it back up with a 28–21 win over the Cleveland Rams on Thanksgiving Day in 1945. Detroit has played on every Thanksgiving Day since.

Bobby Layne. The Lions won four division titles and three league championships between 1952 and 1957. However, Lions fans are still waiting for the team's first Super Bowl appearance.

GREATEST PLAYERS

- **Lem Barney**, DB (1967–77)
- **Dutch Clark**, QB-K (1931–32, 1934–38)
- **Calvin Johnson**, WR (2007–15)
- **Alex Karras**, DT (1958–70)
- **Yale Lary**, DB-P (1952–53, 1956–64)
- **Bobby Layne**, QB (1950–58)
- **Dick LeBeau**, DB (1959–72)
- **Barry Sanders**, RB (1989–98)
- **Joe Schmidt**, LB (1953–65)
- **Billy Sims**, RB (1980–84)
- **Matthew Stafford**, QB (2009–20)
- **Doak Walker**, HB-K-P (1950–55)

Running back Barry Sanders took the league by storm as a rookie in 1989.

TEAM STATS AND RECORDS

ALL-TIME RECORD

- **Regular Season**: 567–681–33
- **Postseason**: 7–13
- **Super Bowl Record**: 0–0

Receiver Calvin Johnson was an explosive threat for the Lions.

TOP COACHES

- **George Wilson** (1957–64); 53–45–6 (regular season); 2–0, 1 NFL title (postseason)
- **Wayne Fontes** (1988–96); 66–67 (regular season); 1–4 (postseason)

CAREER OFFENSIVE LEADERS

- **Games played:** Dominic Raiola, 219
- **Passing yards:** Matthew Stafford, 45,109
- **Passing TDs:** Matthew Stafford, 282
- **Rushing yards:** Barry Sanders, 15,269
- **Rushing TDs:** Barry Sanders, 99
- **Receiving yards:** Calvin Johnson, 11,619
- **Receiving TDs:** Calvin Johnson, 83

CAREER DEFENSIVE LEADERS

- **Games played:** Wayne Walker, 200
- **Sacks:** Robert Porcher, 95.5
- **Tackles:** Chris Spielman, 1,020
- **Interceptions:** Dick LeBeau, 62
- **Fumble recoveries:** Lem Barney, Joe Schmidt, and Chris Spielman, 17

CAREER SPECIAL TEAMS LEADERS

- **Yards per punt:** Sam Martin, 46.0
- **Field goals:** Jason Hansen, 495
- **Field goal percentage:** Matt Prater, 84.4

GREATEST SEASONS

The Detroit Lions won their most recent championship in 1957. That team started the season 5–4, and star quarterback Layne was injured. But backup Tobin Rote guided the Lions to victories in their final three games, forcing a one-game playoff to decide the West Division. The Lions traveled to San Francisco. They fell behind the 49ers 27–7 in the third quarter. But Rote led a stunning comeback. He rallied Detroit to a 31–27 win. The next week, Rote threw for 280 yards and four touchdowns. The Lions blew out the Browns for the title. The next season, the team shipped Layne to Pittsburgh. He was angry with the trade. On the way out the door, he supposedly said the team wouldn't win another title for 50 years. By 2020 Detroit had won just one of 13 playoff games since the trade.

Quarterback Tobin Rote (18) throws a pass against the Browns in the 1957 NFL Championship Game.

TEAM HISTORY

The Green Bay Packers joined the APFA in 1921. They were an early power under coach Curly Lambeau, winning six league titles between 1929 and 1944. Vince Lombardi took over as head coach in 1959. He led the Packers to five more championships, including victories in the first two Super Bowls. After a long dry spell, quarterback Brett Favre and head coach Mike Holmgren made the Packers regular playoff participants in the 1990s and won another Super Bowl. When Favre left after the 2007 season, Aaron Rodgers took over. He won another title along with three NFL MVP Awards.

Packers quarterback Aaron Rodgers emerged as one of the NFL's greatest passers ever.

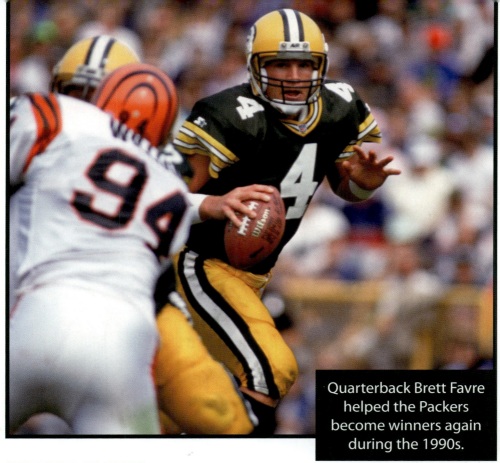

Quarterback Brett Favre helped the Packers become winners again during the 1990s.

GREATEST PLAYERS

- **Herb Adderley**, CB (1961–69)
- **LeRoy Butler**, DB (1990–2001)
- **Brett Favre**, QB (1992–2007)
- **Forrest Gregg**, T (1956, 1958–70)
- **Paul Hornung**, RB (1957–62, 1964–66)
- **Don Hutson**, WR (1935–45)
- **Ray Nitschke**, LB (1958–72)
- **Aaron Rodgers**, QB (2005–)
- **Bart Starr**, QB (1956–71)
- **Jim Taylor**, FB (1958–66)
- **Reggie White**, DE (1993–98)
- **Willie Wood**, DB (1960–71)

TEAM STATS AND RECORDS

ALL-TIME RECORD

- **Regular Season:** 769–577–38
- **Postseason:** 36–24
- **Super Bowl Record:** 4–1

TOP COACHES

- **Curly Lambeau** (1921–49); 209–104–21 (regular season); 3–2, 6 NFL titles (postseason)
- **Vince Lombardi** (1959–67); 89–29–4 (regular season); 9–1, 3 NFL titles, 2 Super Bowl titles (postseason)
- **Mike McCarthy** (2006–18); 125–77–2 (regular season); 10–8, 1 Super Bowl title (postseason)

Coach Vince Lombardi gets a lift from guard Jerry Kramer after the Packers defeated the Raiders 33–14 in Super Bowl II.

CAREER OFFENSIVE LEADERS

- **Games played:** Brett Favre, 255
- **Passing yards:** Brett Favre, 61,655
- **Passing TDs:** Brett Favre, 442
- **Rushing yards:** Ahman Green, 8,322
- **Rushing TDs:** Jim Taylor, 81
- **Receiving yards:** Donald Driver, 10,137
- **Receiving TDs:** Don Hutson, 99

CAREER DEFENSIVE LEADERS

- **Games played:** Ray Nitschke, 190
- **Sacks:** Clay Matthews, 83.5
- **Tackles:** LeRoy Butler, 720
- **Interceptions:** Bobby Dillon, 52
- **Fumble recoveries:** Ray Nitschke, 23

CAREER SPECIAL TEAMS LEADERS

- **Yards per punt:** JK Scott, 44.6
- **Field goals:** Mason Crosby, 345
- **Field goal percentage:** Mason Crosby, 81.8

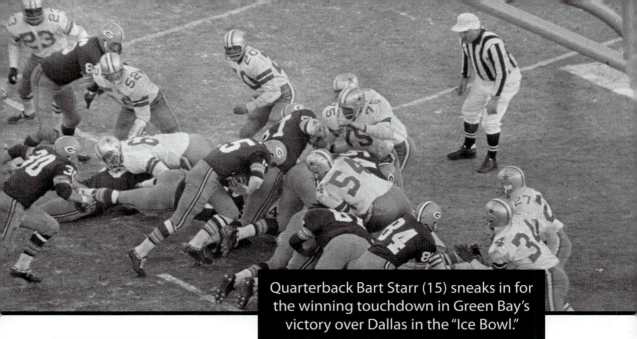

Quarterback Bart Starr (15) sneaks in for the winning touchdown in Green Bay's victory over Dallas in the "Ice Bowl."

GREATEST SEASONS

The Packers won the first Super Bowl after the 1966 season. But in 1967 the veterans of the Lombardi dynasty were beginning to show their age. The team lost four games but still won its division. And after beating the Los Angeles Rams in the first round of the playoffs, the Packers faced the Dallas Cowboys in the championship game. The game became known as the "Ice Bowl" due to the freezing temperatures and frozen turf at Lambeau Field. Quarterback Bart Starr scored on a dive play with seconds left. He gave Green Bay a 21–17 victory. The Packers then crushed the Oakland Raiders in Super Bowl II. That was Lombardi's last game as head coach.

SOLD-OUT GAMES

Season tickets for the Packers are famously hard to get. Lambeau Field has sold out every game since 1960. The only way to get tickets is for fans to place their names on the team's waiting list. In 2020, that list had more than 130,000 names. Many parents add their children's names to the list as soon as they are born. But only a few hundred new people get tickets each year. That means most fans will never get the chance at season tickets.

HOUSTON TEXANS

TEAM HISTORY

The Houston Texans entered the NFL in 2002. They replaced the Houston Oilers, who moved to Tennessee in 1997. The Texans started out on the right foot, winning their regular-season opener against the Dallas Cowboys. But they went just 4–12 that year and didn't get their first winning season until 2009. Then they won six division titles between 2011 and 2019. This gave Houston football fans hope that big-time success was just around the corner.

GREATEST PLAYERS

- **David Carr**, QB (2002–06)
- **Brian Cushing**, LB (2009–17)
- **Owen Daniels**, TE (2006–13)
- **Arian Foster**, RB (2009–15)
- **Aaron Glenn**, CB (2002–04)
- **DeAndre Hopkins**, WR (2013–19)
- **Andre Johnson**, WR (2003–14)
- **Dunta Robinson**, CB (2004–09)
- **DeMeco Ryans**, LB (2006–11)
- **Matt Schaub**, QB (2007–13)
- **J. J. Watt**, DE (2011–20)
- **Mario Williams**, DE (2006–11)

RING OF HONOR

The Texans were the newest team in the NFL as of 2021. They have their own way to pay tribute to their players. The team has a Ring of Honor. It began in 2017 when standout wide receiver Andre Johnson was inducted.

Mario Williams helped beef up the defense after the Texans chose him with the first pick in the 2006 NFL Draft.

TEAM STATS AND RECORDS

ALL-TIME RECORD
- **Regular Season:** 135–169
- **Postseason:** 4–6
- **Super Bowl Record:** 0–0

TOP COACHES
- **Gary Kubiak** (2006–13); 61–64 (regular season); 2–2 (postseason)
- **Bill O'Brien** (2014–20); 52–48 (regular season); 2–4 (postseason)

CAREER OFFENSIVE LEADERS
- **Games played:** Andre Johnson, 169
- **Passing yards:** Matt Schaub, 23,221
- **Passing TDs:** Matt Schaub, 124
- **Rushing yards:** Arian Foster, 6,472
- **Rushing TDs:** Arian Foster, 54
- **Receiving yards:** Andre Johnson, 13,597
- **Receiving TDs:** Andre Johnson, 64

CAREER DEFENSIVE LEADERS
- **Games played:** Johnathan Joseph, 133
- **Sacks:** J. J. Watt, 101
- **Tackles:** DeMeco Ryans, 479
- **Interceptions:** Johnathan Joseph, 17
- **Fumble recoveries:** J. J. Watt, 16

CAREER SPECIAL TEAMS LEADERS
- **Yards per punt:** Shane Lechler, 47.6
- **Field goals:** Kris Brown, 172
- **Field goal percentage:** Neil Rackers, 86.8

Andre Johnson was one of the NFL's top receivers for more than a decade.

70

GREATEST SEASONS

In 2011, the Texans had the AFC's second-ranked defense. They also had a dynamic running back in Arian Foster. That season, the Texans won ten of their first 13 games. They clinched their first playoff berth with a win at Cincinnati in early December. Even three straight losses to end the regular season didn't dampen the enthusiasm for the Texans in Houston. Fans packed Reliant Stadium for the team's first-ever playoff game on January 7, 2012. It was a rematch against Cincinnati. The score was tied 10–10 late in the first half. Then defensive end J. J. Watt batted a pass into the air at the line of scrimmage. He caught the deflection and returned the ball 29 yards for a touchdown. Late in the fourth quarter, Foster got a 42-yard touchdown run. It sealed a 31–10 victory for the Texans in their playoff debut.

Arian Foster, *left*, was a big part of the Texans' first playoff push.

INDIANAPOLIS COLTS

TEAM HISTORY

The Colts trace their roots to Baltimore, where they were founded in 1953. Quarterback Johnny Unitas led them to two NFL titles in the late 1950s. They won the first Super Bowl after the AFL and NFL merged in 1970. They didn't have much success after that, though. So team owner Robert Irsay moved them to Indianapolis, Indiana, in 1984.

The Colts joined the NFL's elite teams when they drafted quarterback Peyton Manning in 1998. Manning led them to the playoffs 11 times in 13 seasons, and they won the Super Bowl after the 2006 season. Later, quarterback Andrew Luck had some great seasons, but injuries forced him to retire after just seven years.

Colts wide receiver T. Y. Hilton catches a touchdown pass against the Buffalo Bills in 2018.

GREATEST PLAYERS

- **Raymond Berry**, WR (1955–67)
- **Art Donovan**, DT (1953–61)
- **Marvin Harrison**, WR (1996–2008)
- **Edgerrin James**, RB (1999–2005)
- **Bert Jones**, QB (1973–81)
- **Andrew Luck**, QB (2012–16, 2018)
- **John Mackey**, TE (1963–71)
- **Peyton Manning**, QB (1998–2010)
- **Robert Mathis**, DE (2003–16)
- **Lenny Moore**, RB (1956–67)
- **Johnny Unitas**, QB (1956–72)
- **Reggie Wayne**, WR (2001–14)

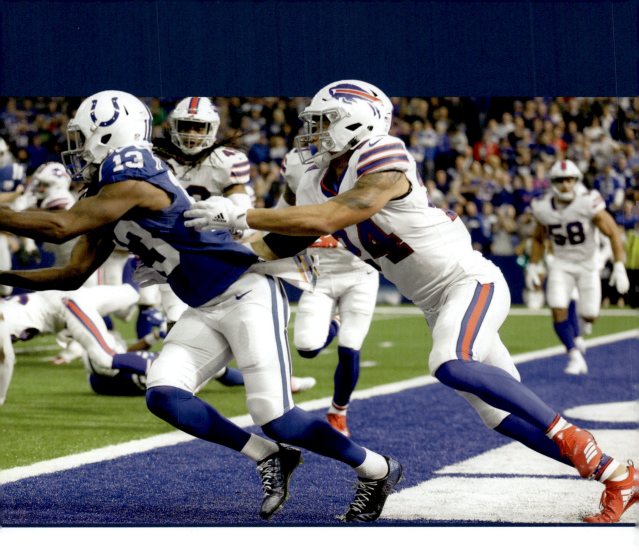

STARTING QUARTERBACKS

From 1998 to 2010, Peyton Manning started every game for the Colts. Other NFL teams have not been as fortunate. During that span, the other 31 NFL teams combined used almost 200 different starting quarterbacks. The Chicago Bears started 17 different players at quarterback between 1998 and 2010. The Cleveland Browns and Miami Dolphins each used 16 different starting quarterbacks during that time.

TEAM STATS AND RECORDS

ALL-TIME RECORD
- **Regular Season**: 534–473–7
- **Postseason**: 23–25
- **Super Bowl Record**: 2–2

TOP COACHES
- **Ted Marchibroda** (1975–79, 1992–95); 71–67 (regular season); 2–4 (postseason)
- **Tony Dungy** (2002–08); 85–27 (regular season); 7–6, 1 Super Bowl title (postseason)

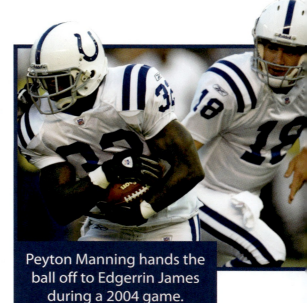

Peyton Manning hands the ball off to Edgerrin James during a 2004 game.

CAREER OFFENSIVE LEADERS
- **Games played**: Reggie Wayne, 211
- **Passing yards**: Peyton Manning, 54,828
- **Passing TDs**: Peyton Manning, 399
- **Rushing yards**: Edgerrin James, 9,226
- **Rushing TDs**: Edgerrin James, 64
- **Receiving yards**: Marvin Harrison, 14,580
- **Receiving TDs**: Marvin Harrison, 128

CAREER DEFENSIVE LEADERS
- **Games played**: Eugene Daniel, 198
- **Sacks**: Robert Mathis, 123
- **Tackles**: Duane Bickett, 1,052
- **Interceptions**: Bobby Boyd, 57
- **Fumble recoveries**: Bruce Laird and Robert Mathis, 17

CAREER SPECIAL TEAMS LEADERS
- **Yards per punt**: Pat McAfee, 46.4
- **Field goals**: Adam Vinatieri, 336
- **Field goal percentage**: Mike Vanderjagt, 87.5

GREATEST SEASONS

The Colts headed into the 2006 season after a string of playoff disappointments. They'd been knocked out twice by Tom Brady and the New England Patriots. In 2005 they had the league's best record, but they were upset at home by the Pittsburgh Steelers. Finally, in 2006, Manning, wide receiver Marvin Harrison, and running back Joseph Addai put it all together. They won their first nine games, including a nationally televised win at New England. In the playoffs, they handled the Chiefs and Ravens before facing the Patriots again. After trailing 21–3 in the second quarter, the Colts staged a furious comeback. Addai's short touchdown run with a minute left gave them a 38–34 victory. In the Super Bowl, the Colts beat the Chicago Bears 29–17.

Indianapolis cornerback Kelvin Hayden intercepts a crucial pass in the fourth quarter of Super Bowl XLI.

The Jaguars hoped Trevor Lawrence could turn them into winners after they picked him first overall in the 2021 draft.

TEAM HISTORY

The Jacksonville Jaguars came into the league in 1995. It didn't take them long to make a name for themselves. They reached the AFC Championship Game in just their second season. It was the first of four straight playoff runs for the young team. They've endured some tough times since then, however. They made only three more playoff appearances between 2000 and 2020.

A BLOWOUT GAME

The Jaguars' 62–7 playoff win over the Miami Dolphins in January 2000 was one of the biggest blowouts in playoff history. The 62 points and 55-point margin of victory both placed second in NFL playoff history. Only the Chicago Bears' 73–0 win over Washington in the 1940 NFL Championship Game was more lopsided.

GREATEST PLAYERS

- **Tony Boselli**, OT (1995–2001)
- **Tony Brackens**, DE (1996–2003)
- **Mark Brunell**, QB (1995–2003)
- **Donovin Darius**, S (1998–2006)
- **David Garrard**, QB (2002–10)
- **Maurice Jones-Drew**, RB (2006–13)
- **Rashean Mathis**, CB (2003–12)
- **Keenan McCardell**, WR (1996–2001)
- **Jalen Ramsey**, CB (2016–19)
- **Jimmy Smith**, WR (1995–2005)
- **Marcus Stroud**, DT (2001–07)
- **Fred Taylor**, RB (1998–2008)

Fred Taylor breaks a tackle in a 1999 game against the Cincinnati Bengals.

TEAM STATS AND RECORDS

ALL-TIME RECORD
- **Regular Season**: 177–239
- **Postseason**: 7–7
- **Super Bowl Record**: 0–0

TOP COACHES
- **Tom Coughlin** (1995–2002); 68–60 (regular season); 4–4 (postseason)
- **Jack Del Rio** (2003–11); 68–71 (regular season); 1–2 (postseason)

CAREER OFFENSIVE LEADERS
- **Games played**: Brad Meester, 209
- **Passing yards**: Mark Brunell, 25,698
- **Passing TDs**: Mark Brunell, 144
- **Rushing yards**: Fred Taylor, 11,271
- **Rushing TDs**: Maurice Jones-Drew, 68
- **Receiving yards**: Jimmy Smith, 12,287
- **Receiving TDs**: Jimmy Smith, 67

CAREER DEFENSIVE LEADERS
- **Games played**: Rob Meier, 138
- **Sacks**: Tony Brackens, 55
- **Tackles**: Paul Posluszny, 587
- **Interceptions**: Rashean Mathis, 30
- **Fumble recoveries**: Tony Brackens, 13

CAREER SPECIAL TEAMS LEADERS
- **Yards per punt**: Bryan Anger, 46.8
- **Field goals**: Josh Scobee, 235
- **Field goal percentage**: Josh Lambo, 95.0

Mark Brunell led the Jaguars into hostile territory when they faced the Broncos in the playoffs in January 1997.

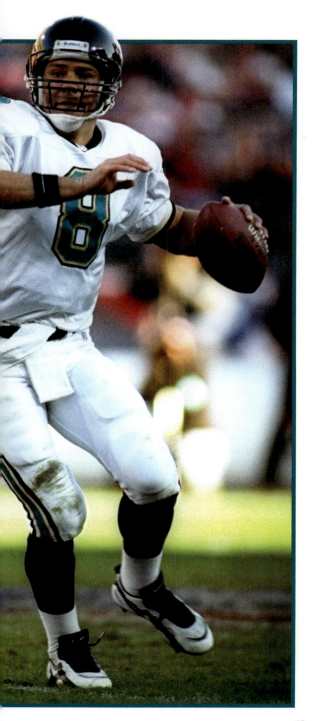

GREATEST SEASONS

The Jaguars entered the 1996 season looking to improve on a 4–12 record. They got off to a shaky start at 4–7. The turning point was a game in late November at Baltimore. Jacksonville trailed 25–10 in the fourth quarter. A loss would have meant that the Jaguars almost certainly would not make the playoffs. But two touchdown passes by Mark Brunell helped them tie the game. Then Mike Hollis made a 34-yard field goal in overtime to give Jacksonville a 28–25 win.

Jacksonville went on to win its final four regular-season games to reach the playoffs at 9–7. Then the Jaguars made a remarkable playoff run, with victories at heavily favored Buffalo and Denver before falling to New England in the AFC Championship Game. In just their second season in the NFL, the Jaguars came within one win of reaching the Super Bowl.

KANSAS CITY CHIEFS

TEAM HISTORY

The Chiefs began as the Dallas Texans in 1960. They were one of the eight original franchises in the AFL. In their third season, the Texans won the AFL Championship. But rather than continue to compete with the NFL's Dallas Cowboys, owner Lamar Hunt moved the team to Kansas City, Missouri. The newly named Chiefs won two more AFL titles. They also represented the league in two of the first four Super Bowls. The Chiefs lost to the Green Bay Packers in the inaugural big game. But they defeated the Minnesota Vikings in Super Bowl IV. Despite a number of close calls over the years, the Chiefs didn't make it back to the Super Bowl until quarterback Patrick Mahomes led them to the title in 2019.

LAMAR HUNT

Few people believed the AFL could survive. But after six seasons, the league was still growing. Chiefs owner Lamar Hunt was a big reason for the AFL's success. "Hunt was the cornerstone, the integrity of the league. Without him, there would have been no AFL," said former Boston Patriots owner William Sullivan. Sullivan made his remarks at Hunt's induction into the Pro Football Hall of Fame in 1972.

GREATEST PLAYERS

- **Bobby Bell**, DE-LB (1963–74)
- **Buck Buchanan**, DT (1963–75)
- **Len Dawson**, QB (1962–75)
- **Tony Gonzalez**, TE (1997–2008)
- **Abner Haynes**, HB (1960–64)
- **Travis Kelce**, TE (2013–)
- **Willie Lanier**, LB (1967–77)
- **Patrick Mahomes**, QB, 2017–)
- **Ed Podolak**, RB (1969–77)
- **Otis Taylor**, WR (1965–75)
- **Derrick Thomas**, LB (1989–99)
- **Emmitt Thomas**, CB (1966–78)

Patrick Mahomes took the NFL by storm after securing the Chiefs' starting quarterback job in 2018.

TEAM STATS AND RECORDS

ALL-TIME RECORD

- **Regular Season:** 495–425–12
- **Postseason:** 15–20
- **Super Bowl Record:** 2–2

TOP COACHES

- **Hank Stram** (1960–74); 124–76–10 (regular season); 5–3, 2 AFL titles, 1 Super Bowl title (postseason)
- **Marty Schottenheimer** (1989–98); 101–58–1 (regular season); 3–7 (postseason)

CAREER OFFENSIVE LEADERS

- **Games played:** Will Shields, 224
- **Passing yards:** Len Dawson, 28,507
- **Passing TDs:** Len Dawson, 237
- **Rushing yards:** Jamaal Charles, 7,260
- **Rushing TDs:** Priest Holmes, 76
- **Receiving yards:** Tony Gonzalez, 10,940
- **Receiving TDs:** Tony Gonzalez, 76

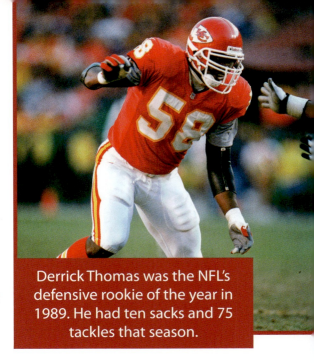

Derrick Thomas was the NFL's defensive rookie of the year in 1989. He had ten sacks and 75 tackles that season.

CAREER DEFENSIVE LEADERS

- **Games played:** Buck Buchanan, 182
- **Sacks:** Derrick Thomas, 126.5
- **Tackles:** Derrick Johnson, 941
- **Interceptions:** Emmitt Thomas, 58
- **Fumble recoveries:** Derrick Thomas, 19

CAREER SPECIAL TEAMS LEADERS

- **Yards per punt:** Dustin Colquitt, 44.8
- **Field goals:** Nick Lowery, 329
- **Field goal percentage:** Harrison Butker, 90.3

GREATEST SEASONS

In 2018 the Chiefs nearly won it all under first-year starter Mahomes. But the NFL MVP lost an epic duel with Tom Brady and the New England Patriots in the AFC title game. The Chiefs would not be denied in 2019, however. They won their final six regular-season games to clinch the second seed in the AFC playoffs. Then they coasted past the Texans and Titans. Finally, Mahomes led a furious 21-point rally in the fourth quarter of the Super Bowl. The Chiefs beat the 49ers 31–20. This put Kansas City on top of the football world.

Tight end Tony Gonzalez went to ten straight Pro Bowls during his 12-year career with the Chiefs.

TEAM HISTORY

Few teams in pro sports history have bounced around more than the Raiders. They started out in Oakland, California, in 1960. They stayed there until 1982. That's when owner Al Davis moved them to Los Angeles. Davis then brought them back to Oakland in 1995. But stadium problems drove them away in 2020, and they moved

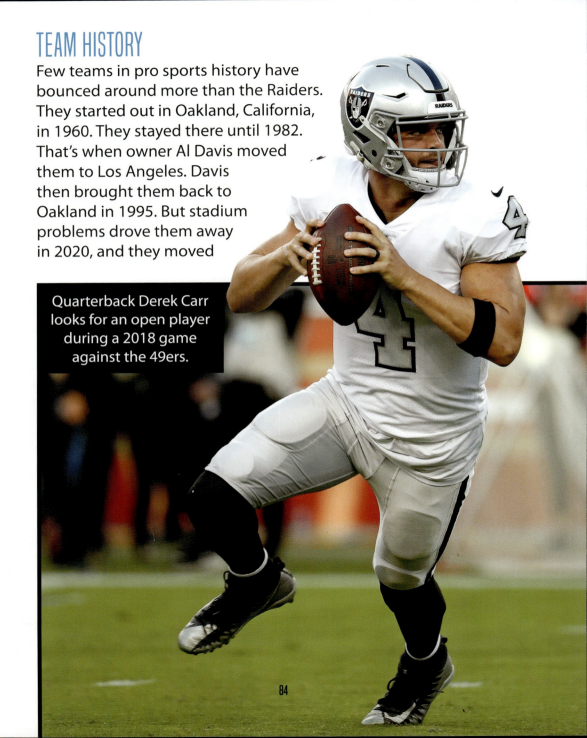

Quarterback Derek Carr looks for an open player during a 2018 game against the 49ers.

Tim Brown breaks loose for a touchdown against the Chargers in 1988.

to Las Vegas, Nevada. Along the way, the Raiders put together a few dominant eras. They reached the playoffs 15 times between 1967 and 1985. The Raiders won the Super Bowl three times in that stretch. But they missed the playoffs in 16 of their final 17 seasons in Oakland. Raiders fans hoped the move to Las Vegas would breathe new life into their team.

GREATEST PLAYERS

- **Marcus Allen**, RB (1982–92)
- **Fred Biletnikoff**, WR (1965–78)
- **Tim Brown**, WR (1988–2003)
- **Willie Brown**, DB (1967–78)
- **Derek Carr**, QB (2014–)
- **Dave Casper**, TE (1974–80, 1984)
- **Howie Long**, DE (1981–93)
- **Jim Otto**, C (1960–74)
- **Art Shell**, T (1968–82)
- **Ken Stabler**, QB (1970–79)
- **Jack Tatum**, S (1971–79)
- **Gene Upshaw**, G (1967–81)

TEAM STATS AND RECORDS

ALL-TIME RECORD

- **Regular Season:** 481–440–11
- **Postseason:** 25–19
- **Super Bowl Record:** 3–2

TOP COACHES

- **John Madden** (1969–78); 103–32–7 (regular season); 9–7, 1 Super Bowl title (postseason)
- **Tom Flores** (1979–87); 83–53 (regular season); 8–3, 2 Super Bowl titles (postseason)

CAREER OFFENSIVE LEADERS

- **Games played:** Tim Brown, 240
- **Passing yards:** Derek Carr, 26,896
- **Passing TDs:** Derek Carr, 170
- **Rushing yards:** Marcus Allen, 8,545
- **Rushing TDs:** Marcus Allen, 79
- **Receiving yards:** Tim Brown, 14,734
- **Receiving TDs:** Tim Brown, 99

AL DAVIS AND THE RAIDERS

Owner Al Davis had a personal philosophy for running the Raiders. "We want to win," he said. "The Raider fans deserve it. The Raider players deserve it, even my organization deserves it. You have to win and you have to win with a vision for the Super Bowl. That's our passion here."

CAREER DEFENSIVE LEADERS

- **Games played:** Howie Long, 179
- **Sacks:** Greg Townsend, 107.5
- **Tackles:** Eddie Anderson, 761
- **Interceptions:** Lester Hayes and Willie Brown, 39
- **Fumble recoveries:** Phil Villapiano, 17

CAREER SPECIAL TEAMS LEADERS

- **Yards per punt:** Shane Lechler, 47.5
- **Field goals:** Sebastian Janikowski, 414
- **Field goal percentage:** Daniel Carlson, 87.2

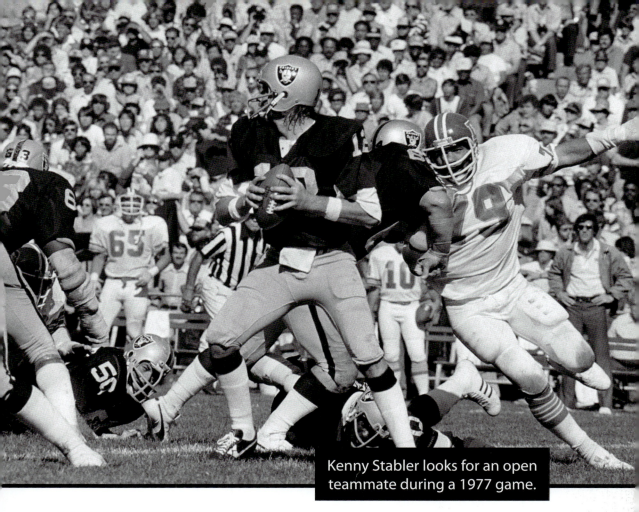

Kenny Stabler looks for an open teammate during a 1977 game.

GREATEST SEASONS

The Raiders dominated the NFL in 1976. Only one loss against New England kept them from going undefeated. Quarterback Ken Stabler, wide receiver Cliff Branch, and tight end Dave Casper led an offense that averaged 25 points a game. On defense, linebackers Phil Villapiano and Ted Hendricks kept opposing offenses in check. Hard-hitting safeties Jack Tatum and George Atkinson patrolled the secondary. In the playoffs, the Raiders got revenge on the Patriots with a 24–21 win. Then they defeated the Steelers—who were two-time Super Bowl champions—24–7 to win the AFC title. A 32–14 victory over the Vikings in the Super Bowl was the perfect ending for one of the NFL's all-time great seasons.

LOS ANGELES CHARGERS

TEAM HISTORY

In 1960, the Los Angeles Chargers were one of eight teams to kick off the first season of the AFL. But after reaching the AFL Championship Game in their first season, the Chargers moved down the Pacific coast to San Diego, California. They were no longer competing with the NFL's Los Angeles Rams for attention, and the Chargers continued to thrive on the field. They reached the AFL title game four more times in the next five years, winning it in 1963. The offenses of the late 1970s and early 1980s helped the Chargers win three straight AFC West titles. Since then, it's been hit-or-miss for the Chargers, who moved back to Los Angeles in 2017 in search of a better stadium deal.

Wide receiver Keenan Allen made his fourth consecutive Pro Bowl in 2020.

GREATEST PLAYERS

- **Lance Alworth**, WR (1962–70)
- **Fred Dean**, DE (1975–81)
- **Dan Fouts**, QB (1973–87)
- **Antonio Gates**, TE (2003–18)
- **John Hadl**, QB (1962–72)
- **Charlie Joiner**, WR (1976–86)
- **Keith Lincoln**, RB (1961–66, 1968)

- **Philip Rivers**, QB (2004–19)
- **Junior Seau**, LB (1990–2002)
- **LaDainian Tomlinson**, RB (2001–09)
- **Eric Weddle**, S (2007–15)
- **Kellen Winslow**, TE (1979–87)

The Chargers' Junior Seau (55) makes a tackle in the AFC Championship Game in January 1995.

LOS ANGELES CHARGERS

TEAM STATS AND RECORDS

ALL-TIME RECORD
- **Regular Season:** 459–462–11
- **Postseason:** 12–18
- **Super Bowl Record:** 0–1

TOP COACHES
- **Sid Gillman** (1960–69, 1971); 86–53–6 (regular season); 1–4, 1 AFL title (postseason)
- **Don Coryell** (1978–86); 69–56 (regular season); 3–4 (postseason)

CAREER OFFENSIVE LEADERS
- **Games played:** Antonio Gates, 236
- **Passing yards:** Philip Rivers, 59,271
- **Passing TDs:** Philip Rivers, 397
- **Rushing yards:** LaDainian Tomlinson, 12,490
- **Rushing TDs:** LaDainian Tomlinson, 138
- **Receiving yards:** Antonio Gates, 11,841
- **Receiving TDs:** Antonio Gates, 116

CAREER DEFENSIVE LEADERS
- **Games played:** Junior Seau, 200
- **Sacks:** Leslie O'Neal, 105.5
- **Tackles:** Junior Seau, 1,287
- **Interceptions:** Gill Byrd, 42
- **Fumble recoveries:** Junior Seau, 16

CAREER SPECIAL TEAMS LEADERS
- **Yards per punt:** Drew Kaser, 47.4
- **Field goals:** John Carney, 261
- **Field goal percentage:** Nate Kaeding, 87.0

GREATEST SEASONS

The 1994 Chargers rolled to an 11–5 record and a division title. Running back Natrone Means rushed for 1,350 yards and 12 touchdowns. Linebacker Junior Seau and defensive end Leslie O'Neal paced the defense. The Chargers traveled to Pittsburgh for the AFC Championship Game. They pulled off a 17–13 upset before falling to the San Francisco 49ers in their first Super Bowl appearance.

CHARGERS IN THE PLAYOFFS

The Chargers' 41–38 overtime victory in Miami on January 2, 1982, remains one of the greatest playoff games in NFL history. The Chargers jumped to a 24–0 lead in the first quarter. The Dolphins surged back to take the lead. Then the Chargers tied the score with 58 seconds left in regulation. Both teams missed field goals in overtime. Finally, Rolf Benirschke kicked a 29-yard field goal to win it for the Chargers.

LOS ANGELES RAMS

Aaron Donald helped rebuild the Rams' reputation for defense.

TEAM HISTORY

The Rams have called three different cities home over the years. They formed in Cleveland in 1937. In 1945, they won the NFL title. Then they moved to Los Angeles. This move made them the first major professional sports team in California. The Rams made four trips to the title game in their first decade in Los Angeles, winning it once. They built a strong defensive squad behind a line nicknamed the "Fearsome Foursome." But despite winning seven straight division titles, they kept falling short. They reached the Super Bowl just once and lost to Pittsburgh. In 1995, the team moved to St. Louis, Missouri. It struggled until quarterback Kurt Warner led the team to a title in 1999. After 21 years in St. Louis, the Rams returned to Los Angeles in 2016. Two years later, they reached another Super Bowl but lost to New England.

GREATEST PLAYERS

- **Isaac Bruce**, WR (1994–2007)
- **Eric Dickerson**, RB (1983–87)
- **Aaron Donald**, DT (2014–)
- **Marshall Faulk**, RB (1999–2005)
- **Elroy Hirsch**, RB-WR (1949–57)
- **Deacon Jones**, DE (1961–71)
- **Merlin Olsen**, DT (1962–76)
- **Jackie Slater**, OT (1976–95)
- **Norm Van Brocklin**, QB (1949–57)
- **Kurt Warner**, QB (1998–2003)
- **Bob Waterfield**, QB (1945–52)
- **Jack Youngblood**, DE (1971–84)

THE RAMS LOGO

The Rams were the first pro team to feature a logo on their helmets. The signature ram horn design on the team's helmets began with running back Fred Gehrke in 1947. Gehrke was an art major in college. He painted the yellow horn on a leather helmet. Eventually he painted 75 helmets, and the team adopted the logo.

Rams running back Marshall Faulk looks for space to run in Super Bowl XXXIV.

93

TEAM STATS AND RECORDS

ALL-TIME RECORD
- **Regular Season**: 587–575–21
- **Postseason**: 22–27
- **Super Bowl Record**: 1–3

TOP COACHES
- **Chuck Knox** (1973–77, 1992–94); 69–48–1 (regular season); 3–5 (postseason)
- **John Robinson** (1983–91); 75–68 (regular season); 4–6 (postseason)

CAREER OFFENSIVE LEADERS
- **Games played:** Jackie Slater, 259
- **Passing yards:** Jim Everett, 23,758
- **Passing TDs:** Roman Gabriel, 154
- **Rushing yards:** Steven Jackson, 10,138
- **Rushing TDs:** Marshall Faulk and Todd Gurley, 58
- **Receiving yards:** Isaac Bruce, 14,109
- **Receiving TDs:** Isaac Bruce, 84

CAREER DEFENSIVE LEADERS
- **Games played:** Merlin Olsen, 208
- **Sacks:** Leonard Little, 87.5
- **Tackles:** James Laurinaitis, 655
- **Interceptions:** Eddie Meador, 46
- **Fumble recoveries:** Eddie Meador and Johnnie Johnson, 22

CAREER SPECIAL TEAMS LEADERS
- **Yards per punt:** Johnny Hekker, 46.9
- **Field goals:** Jeff Wilkins, 265
- **Field goal percentage:** Greg Zuerlein, 82.0

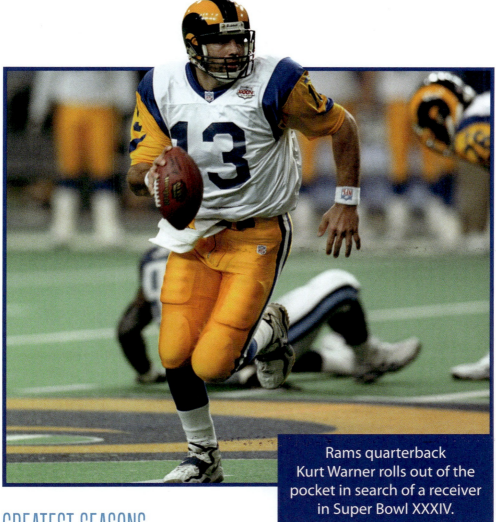

Rams quarterback Kurt Warner rolls out of the pocket in search of a receiver in Super Bowl XXXIV.

GREATEST SEASONS

The 1999 Rams were supposed to be led by quarterback Trent Green, but he suffered a season-ending injury in the preseason. His backup was 28-year-old Kurt Warner, who had thrown only 11 NFL passes. But Warner had an amazing season. He led the NFL with 41 touchdown passes and won the league's MVP award. Running back Marshall Faulk was a valuable player too. He rushed for 1,381 yards and caught 87 passes for 1,048 yards. The Rams lost just three games all year. They capped the season with a nail-biting win over the Tennessee Titans for their first Super Bowl trophy.

MIAMI DOLPHINS

TEAM HISTORY

The Dolphins began playing in 1966. They were the first group to join the AFL's original eight teams. Once the leagues merged in 1970, they quickly became a force. The Dolphins won more games in that decade than any other AFC team. The 1972 and 1973 Dolphins won back-to-back Super Bowls behind legendary head coach Don Shula. He coached the team for 26 years. He finished his career with an NFL record of 328 regular-season victories. Hall of Fame quarterback Dan Marino set NFL records for passing yards and touchdown passes.

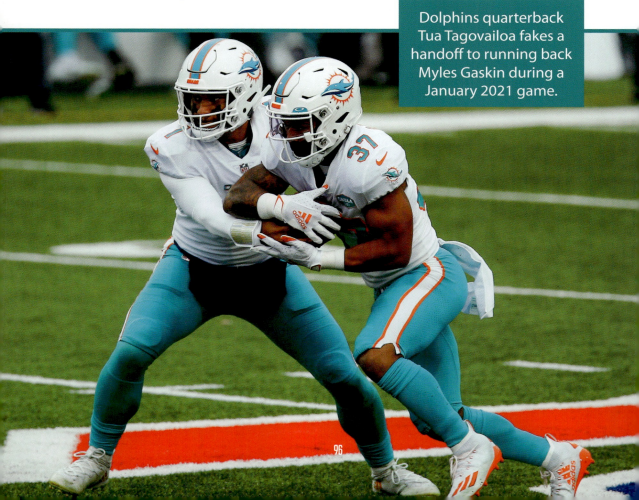

Dolphins quarterback Tua Tagovailoa fakes a handoff to running back Myles Gaskin during a January 2021 game.

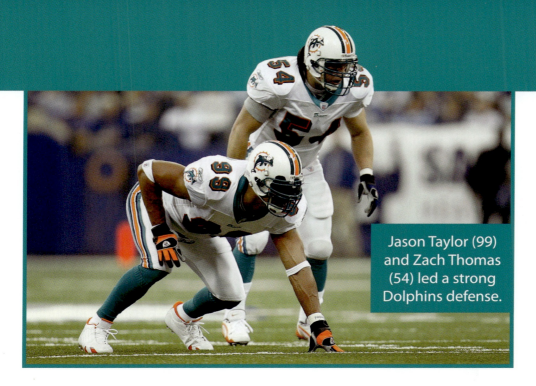

Jason Taylor (99) and Zach Thomas (54) led a strong Dolphins defense.

GREATEST PLAYERS

- **Nick Buoniconti**, LB (1969–76)
- **Mark Clayton**, WR (1983–92)
- **Larry Csonka**, FB (1968–74, 1979)
- **Bob Griese**, QB (1967–80)
- **Bob Kuechenberg**, G (1970–83)
- **Jim Langer**, C (1970–79)
- **Larry Little**, G (1969–80)
- **Dan Marino**, QB (1983–99)
- **Dwight Stephenson**, C (1980–87)
- **Jason Taylor**, DE (1997–2007, 2009, 2011)
- **Zach Thomas**, LB (1996–2007)
- **Richmond Webb**, T (1990–2000)

THE LONGEST GAME

Garo Yepremian kicked a field goal to give the Dolphins a victory over the Kansas City Chiefs on December 25, 1971. But by the time he took the field, fans were starting to wonder if the game would ever end. The teams used 82 minutes and 40 seconds of game time—the longest game in NFL history—to decide the outcome.

TEAM STATS AND RECORDS

ALL-TIME RECORD

- **Regular Season**: 467–377–4
- **Postseason**: 20–21
- **Super Bowl Record**: 2–3

TOP COACHES

- **Don Shula** (1970–95); 257–133–2 (regular season); 17–14, 2 Super Bowl titles (postseason)
- **Dave Wannstedt** (2000–04); 42–31 (regular season); 1–2 (postseason)

CAREER OFFENSIVE LEADERS

- **Games played**: Dan Marino, 242
- **Passing yards**: Dan Marino, 61,361
- **Passing TDs**: Dan Marino, 420
- **Rushing yards**: Larry Csonka, 6,737
- **Rushing TDs**: Larry Csonka, 53
- **Receiving yards**: Mark Duper, 8,869
- **Receiving TDs**: Mark Clayton, 81

CAREER DEFENSIVE LEADERS

- **Games played**: Jason Taylor, 204
- **Sacks**: Jason Taylor, 131
- **Tackles**: Zach Thomas, 1,042
- **Interceptions**: Jake Scott, 35
- **Fumble recoveries**: Jason Taylor, 27

CAREER SPECIAL TEAMS LEADERS

- **Yards per punt**: Brandon Fields, 46.8
- **Field goals**: Olindo Mare, 245
- **Field goal percentage**: Jason Sanders, 86.5

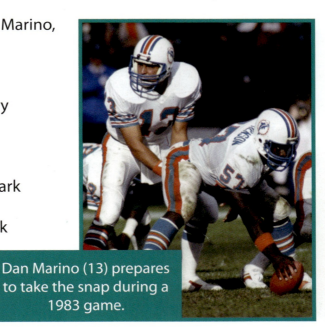

Dan Marino (13) prepares to take the snap during a 1983 game.

GREATEST SEASONS

In 1972, the Dolphins became the first team in the Super Bowl era to have a perfect season. They stormed through their 14-game schedule with relative ease. Only three of their victories were decided by fewer than ten points. Veteran quarterback Earl Morrall won nine games in relief of injured star Bob Griese, who returned for Miami's playoff run. A three-man backfield of fullback Larry Csonka and tailbacks Jim Kiick and Mercury Morris ran wild. They combined for more than 2,600 rushing yards and 23 touchdowns. And the team's "No-Name Defense" was the best in the NFL. A 14–7 victory over Washington in the Super Bowl left the Dolphins 17–0. Through 2020, they remained the only Super Bowl champion with a perfect record.

Earl Morrall filled in just fine for the injured Griese during the Dolphins' perfect 1972 season.

MINNESOTA VIKINGS

Undrafted wide receiver Adam Thielen emerged as one of the top players at his position in 2017.

TEAM HISTORY

The Vikings joined the NFL in 1961. After a slow start, they hired head coach Bud Grant in 1967. They quickly became a force. Grant took the Vikings to four Super Bowls in eight years, although they lost all four. The team was famous for its home field advantage during the playoffs. The cold weather at their stadium often made life difficult for warm-weather opponents. The Vikings moved indoors in 1982. The team is still looking for its first Super Bowl win.

GREATEST PLAYERS

- **Cris Carter**, WR (1990–2001)
- **Carl Eller**, DE (1964–78)
- **Chuck Foreman**, RB (1973–79)
- **Paul Krause**, S (1968–79)
- **Jim Marshall**, DE (1961–79)
- **Randall McDaniel**, G (1988–99)
- **Randy Moss**, WR (1998–2004, 2010)
- **Alan Page**, DT (1967–78)
- **Adrian Peterson**, RB (2007–16)
- **John Randle**, DT (1990–2000)
- **Fran Tarkenton**, QB (1961–66, 1972–78)
- **Mick Tingelhoff**, C (1962–78)

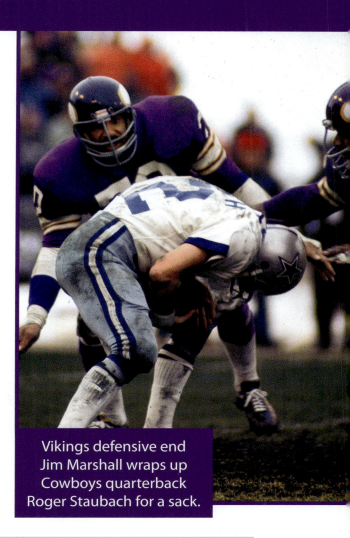

Vikings defensive end Jim Marshall wraps up Cowboys quarterback Roger Staubach for a sack.

FROM THE FOOTBALL FIELD TO THE LAW BENCH

Vikings defensive lineman Alan Page was the NFL's MVP in 1971. This is a rare feat for a defensive player. While Page played professional football, he started law school. He graduated in 1978 and retired from football a few years later. Page became a successful lawyer. He was elected to the Minnesota State Supreme Court in 1992.

TEAM STATS AND RECORDS

ALL-TIME RECORD

- **Regular Season:** 495–412–11
- **Postseason:** 21–30
- **Super Bowl Record:** 0–4

TOP COACHES

- **Bud Grant** (1967–83, 1985); 158–96–5 (regular season); 10–12 (postseason)
- **Dennis Green** (1992–2001); 97–62 (regular season); 4–8 (postseason)

Minnesota quarterback Fran Tarkenton scrambles against the Green Bay Packers in 1966.

CAREER OFFENSIVE LEADERS

- **Games played:** Mick Tingelhoff, 240
- **Passing yards:** Fran Tarkenton, 33,098
- **Passing TDs:** Fran Tarkenton, 239
- **Rushing yards:** Adrian Peterson, 11,747
- **Rushing TDs:** Adrian Peterson, 97
- **Receiving yards:** Cris Carter, 12,383
- **Receiving TDs:** Cris Carter, 110

CAREER DEFENSIVE LEADERS

- **Games played:** Jim Marshall, 270
- **Sacks:** John Randle, 114
- **Tackles:** Carl Lee, 771
- **Interceptions:** Paul Krause, 53
- **Fumble recoveries:** Jim Marshall, 29

CAREER SPECIAL TEAMS LEADERS

- **Yards per punt:** Britton Colquitt, 45.1
- **Field goals:** Fred Cox, 282
- **Field goal percentage:** Ryan Longwell, 86.0

Wide receiver Stefon Diggs scored a game-winning touchdown against New Orleans in January 2018. The play was called the "Minneapolis Miracle."

GREATEST SEASONS

The Vikings' most memorable season might be their remarkable run in 1998. The team went 15–1. The Vikings lost only a Week 9 game at Tampa Bay. On offense was rookie wide receiver Randy Moss and fellow Hall of Famer Cris Carter. The Minnesota offense broke the NFL scoring record. They averaged nearly 35 points per game. They were heavily favored to reach the Super Bowl. However, they suffered a shocking overtime defeat to the Atlanta Falcons in the NFC Championship Game.

NEW ENGLAND PATRIOTS

The Patriots' Stephon Gilmore makes a key interception to help New England beat the Rams in the Super Bowl in February 2019.

TEAM HISTORY

The Boston Patriots were one of the eight original AFL teams. They began playing in 1960. The Patriots didn't have much early success. They reached the playoffs just once in ten AFL seasons. In 1971, they changed their name to the New England Patriots. The longtime losers became the NFL's most dominant dynasty after Bill Belichick was hired as head coach in 2000. The Patriots came out of nowhere with quarterback Tom Brady to win the Super Bowl after the 2001 season. They won five more under Belichick and Brady.

GREATEST PLAYERS

- **Drew Bledsoe**, QB (1993–2001)
- **Tom Brady**, QB (2000–19)
- **Gino Cappelletti**, K-WR (1960–70)
- **Julian Edelman**, WR (2009–20)
- **Steve Grogan**, QB (1975–90)
- **Rob Gronkowski**, TE (2010–18)
- **John Hannah**, G (1973–85)
- **Matt Light**, LT (2001–11)
- **Stanley Morgan**, WR (1977–89)
- **Andre Tippett**, LB (1982–93)
- **Adam Vinatieri**, K (1996–2005)
- **Vince Wilfork**, DT (2004–14)

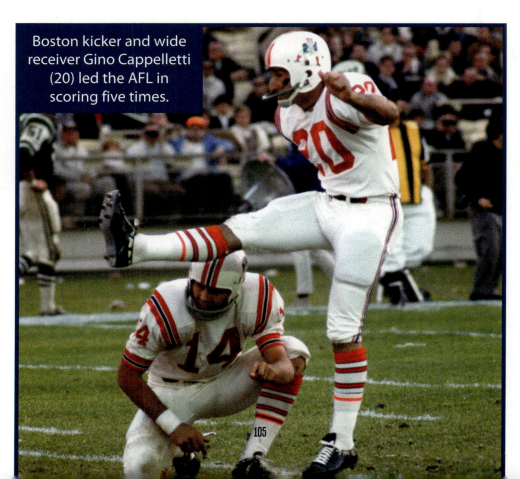

Boston kicker and wide receiver Gino Cappelletti (20) led the AFL in scoring five times.

TEAM STATS AND RECORDS

ALL-TIME RECORD

- **Regular Season**: 519–404–9
- **Postseason**: 37–21
- **Super Bowl Record**: 6–5

TOP COACHES

- **Mike Holovak** (1961–68); 52–46–9 (regular season); 1–1 (postseason)
- **Bill Belichick** (2000–); 244–92 (regular season); 30–11, 6 Super Bowl titles (postseason)

CAREER OFFENSIVE LEADERS

- **Games played**: Tom Brady, 285
- **Passing yards**: Tom Brady, 74,571
- **Passing TDs**: Tom Brady, 541
- **Rushing yards**: Sam Cunningham, 5,453
- **Rushing TDs**: Jim Nance, 45
- **Receiving yards**: Stanley Morgan, 10,352
- **Receiving TDs**: Rob Gronkowski, 79

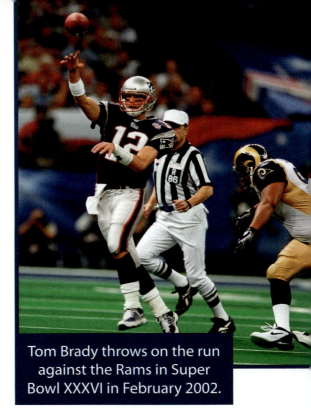

Tom Brady throws on the run against the Rams in Super Bowl XXXVI in February 2002.

CAREER DEFENSIVE LEADERS

- **Games played**: Julius Adams, 206
- **Sacks**: Andre Tippett, 100
- **Tackles**: Vincent Brown, 737
- **Interceptions**: Ty Law and Raymond Clayborn, 36
- **Fumble recoveries**: Andre Tippett, 19

CAREER SPECIAL TEAMS LEADERS

- **Yards per punt**: Jake Bailey, 46.4
- **Field goals**: Stephen Gostkowski, 374
- **Field goal percentage**: Stephen Gostkowski, 87.4

GREATEST SEASONS

The 2007 Patriots played like a team on a mission. The offense set an NFL record. It scored 589 points, or almost 37 points per game. The defense allowed just 17.1 points per game, meaning the Patriots won a lot of blowouts. Brady became the first quarterback to throw 50 touchdown passes in a season. Wide receiver Randy Moss set an NFL record with 23 touchdown receptions. When the Patriots came from behind in the fourth quarter to beat the New York Giants in the final game of the regular season, they became the first NFL team to go 16–0. However, the Giants got their revenge when it counted most. They beat New England 17–14 in the Super Bowl to deny the Patriots a perfect season.

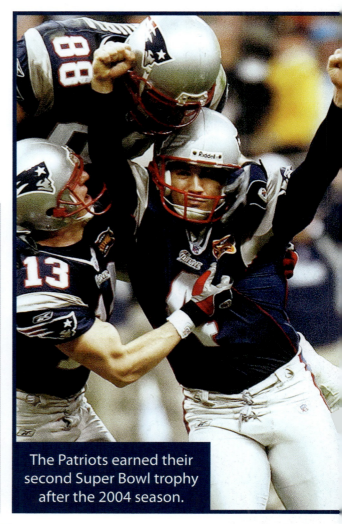

The Patriots earned their second Super Bowl trophy after the 2004 season.

SUCCESS AND SCANDAL

The Patriots' remarkable 2007 season was not without controversy. The NFL disciplined New England after discovering that the team, from its sideline, videotaped the New York Jets defensive coaches' signals during a game on September 9. The league fined head coach Bill Belichick $500,000 and the team $250,000. The league also took away a first-round draft pick in 2008 as punishment for the so-called "spy-gate" scandal.

NEW ORLEANS SAINTS

TEAM HISTORY

The Saints joined the NFL in 1967. They quickly became a punching bag for their opponents. New Orleans didn't have a winning record in any of its first 20 seasons. The Saints finally broke that streak in 1987. They made the playoffs four times in the next six years. But they didn't find playoff success until quarterback Drew Brees arrived in 2006. He wrote his name all over the NFL record book. Brees made the Saints one of the most feared teams in the league.

GREATEST PLAYERS

- **Morten Andersen**, K (1982–94)
- **Drew Brees**, QB (2006–20)
- **Stan Brock**, T (1980–92)
- **Mark Ingram**, RB (2011–18)
- **Rickey Jackson**, LB (1981–93)
- **Alvin Kamara**, RB (2017–)
- **Archie Manning**, QB (1971–82)
- **Deuce McAllister**, RB (2001–08)
- **Sam Mills**, LB (1986–94)
- **William Roaf**, T (1993–2001)
- **Pat Swilling**, LB (1986–92)
- **Michael Thomas**, WR (2016–)

THE FIRST PLAY

The Saints got off to a good start when John Gilliam scored a touchdown on the first play in team history. On September 17, 1967, Gilliam returned the opening kickoff 94 yards for a touchdown against the Los Angeles Rams. "I was a rookie, nervous and afraid," he said. "The football was kicked down the middle. . . . I caught it and took off running. . . . I veered to my left, and I was running free. What a great feeling. What a super feeling!"

GREATEST SEASONS

The 1986 Giants went 14–2. They coasted to a Super Bowl title on the strength of a great defense. Their next Super Bowl victory four years later was a tougher test. Starting quarterback Phil Simms suffered a season-ending injury in mid-December. Backup Jeff Hostetler was untested. However, a strong running game and another defensive effort took some of the pressure off him. A 15–13 upset win at San Francisco gave the Giants the NFC title. In the Super Bowl, New York's game plan focused on ball control. They wanted to keep Buffalo's high-flying offense off the field. It worked. The Giants held the ball for more than two-thirds of the game. A missed field goal at the end let them hold on for a 20–19 victory.

TEAM HISTORY

The New York Titans began play in 1960. They were one of the AFL's founding members. They changed their name to the Jets after three seasons. In 1968, they made the playoffs for the first time. The Jets went all the way, becoming the first AFL team to win the Super Bowl. Through 2020, they hadn't been back to the big game. However, they've had a few close calls. They've also had lots of dry spells. From 2011 to 2020, they posted just one winning season and missed the playoffs every year.

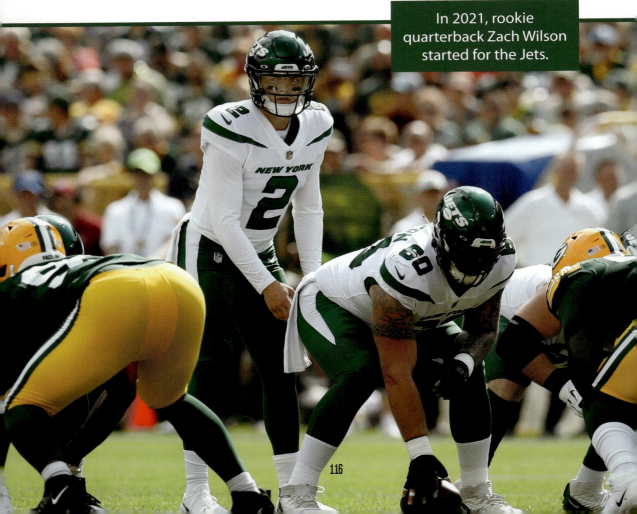

In 2021, rookie quarterback Zach Wilson started for the Jets.

Mark Gastineau was a sacking machine in the 1980s.

GREATEST PLAYERS

- **Wayne Chrebet**, WR (1995–2005)
- **Mark Gastineau**, DE (1979–88)
- **Joe Klecko**, DL (1977–87)
- **Mo Lewis**, LB (1991–2003)
- **Curtis Martin**, RB (1998–2005)
- **Don Maynard**, WR (1960–72)
- **Freeman McNeil**, RB (1981–92)
- **Joe Namath**, QB (1965–76)
- **Darrelle Revis**, CB (2007–12, 2015–16)
- **Matt Snell**, FB (1964–72)
- **Al Toon**, WR (1985–92)
- **Wesley Walker**, WR (1977–89)

TEAM STATS AND RECORDS

ALL-TIME RECORD
- **Regular Season**: 410–514–8
- **Postseason**: 12–13
- **Super Bowl Record**: 1–0

TOP COACHES
- **Weeb Ewbank** (1963–73); 71–77–6 (regular season); 2–1, 1 Super Bowl title (postseason)
- **Joe Walton** (1983–89); 53–57–1 (regular season); 1–2 (postseason)

CAREER OFFENSIVE LEADERS
- **Games played**: Randy Rasmussen, 207
- **Passing yards**: Joe Namath, 27,057
- **Passing TDs**: Joe Namath, 170
- **Rushing yards**: Curtis Martin, 10,302
- **Rushing TDs**: Curtis Martin, 58
- **Receiving yards**: Don Maynard, 11,732
- **Receiving TDs**: Don Maynard, 88

Jets running back Curtis Martin led the NFL with 1,697 rushing yards in 2004.

CAREER DEFENSIVE LEADERS
- **Games played**: Kyle Clifton, 204
- **Sacks**: Mark Gastineau, 74
- **Tackles**: Kyle Clifton, 1,468
- **Interceptions**: Bill Baird, 34
- **Fumble recoveries**: James Hasty, 18

CAREER SPECIAL TEAMS LEADERS
- **Yards per punt**: Lac Edwards, 45.5
- **Field goals**: Pat Leahy, 304
- **Field goal percentage**: Jay Feely, 84.4

GREATEST PLAYERS

- **Eric Allen**, CB (1988–94)
- **Chuck Bednarik**, C-LB (1949–62)
- **Harold Carmichael**, WR (1971–83)
- **Randall Cunningham**, QB (1985–95)
- **Brian Dawkins**, DB (1996–2008)
- **Ron Jaworski**, QB (1977–86)
- **Tommy McDonald**, WR (1957–63)
- **Donovan McNabb**, QB (1999–2009)
- **Jason Peters**, OT (2009–11, 2013–2020)
- **Tra Thomas**, OT (1998–2008)
- **Steve Van Buren**, RB (1944–51)
- **Reggie White**, DE (1985–92)

THE FIRST TELEVISED NFL GAME

The Eagles and the Brooklyn Dodgers played in the first televised NFL game on October 22, 1939. NBC made the game available to the approximately 1,000 television sets in New York City.

Andy Reid, *left*, and Donovan McNabb led the Eagles to many victories.

TEAM STATS AND RECORDS

ALL-TIME RECORD
- **Regular Season**: 590–619–27
- **Postseason**: 23–23
- **Super Bowl Record**: 1–2

TOP COACHES
- **Greasy Neale** (1941–50); 63–43–5 (regular season); 3–1, 2 NFL titles (postseason)
- **Andy Reid** (1999–2012); 130–93–1 (regular season); 10–9 (postseason)

CAREER OFFENSIVE LEADERS
- **Games played:** Harold Carmichael, 180
- **Passing yards:** Donovan McNabb, 32,873
- **Passing TDs:** Donovan McNabb, 216
- **Rushing yards:** LeSean McCoy, 6,792
- **Rushing TDs:** Steve Van Buren, 69
- **Receiving yards:** Harold Carmichael, 8,978
- **Receiving TDs:** Harold Carmichael, 79

CAREER DEFENSIVE LEADERS
- **Games played:** Brian Dawkins, 183
- **Sacks:** Reggie White, 124
- **Tackles:** Andre Waters, 910
- **Interceptions:** Eric Allen, Bill Bradley, and Brian Dawkins, 34
- **Fumble recoveries:** Chuck Bednarik, 21

CAREER SPECIAL TEAMS LEADERS
- **Yards per punt:** Cameron Johnston, 47.0
- **Field goals:** David Akers, 294
- **Field goal percentage:** Alex Henery, 86.0

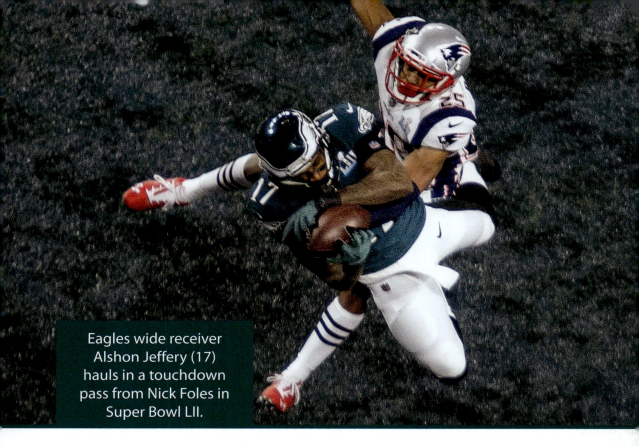

Eagles wide receiver Alshon Jeffery (17) hauls in a touchdown pass from Nick Foles in Super Bowl LII.

GREATEST SEASONS

Going into the 2017 season, the Eagles had made the playoffs just once in the previous six years. They hadn't won a postseason game in nine years. But under second-year quarterback Carson Wentz, they won ten of their first 12 games. Then Wentz got hurt, and the Eagles' prospects dimmed. Little did they know that backup Nick Foles was about to play the best football of his life. Foles helped Philadelphia get home-field advantage with a 13–3 record. Then he threw for 352 yards to beat the Vikings in the NFC title game. The Eagles faced the Patriots in the Super Bowl. Foles had an MVP performance. He passed for 373 yards. He threw three touchdowns. He even caught a touchdown pass. The Eagles got nine points in the final two and a half minutes. They pulled off a 41–33 victory.

PITTSBURGH STEELERS

TEAM HISTORY

The team now known as the Steelers joined the NFL as the Pittsburgh Pirates in 1933. After seven disappointing seasons, they changed to their current nickname. But that didn't help matters much. The Steelers were one of the NFL's least successful teams for their first four decades. In 1969, they hired a defense-minded coach named Chuck Noll. Their fortunes soon turned around. Starting in 1972, they made the playoffs eight straight seasons. They won the Super Bowl four times. Even after that dynasty ended, the Steelers remained one of the NFL's top teams. They regularly made the playoffs. They won two more Super Bowls along the way.

GREATEST PLAYERS

- **Jerome Bettis**, RB (1996–2005)
- **Mel Blount**, CB (1970–83)
- **Terry Bradshaw**, QB (1970–83)
- **Joe Greene**, DT (1969–81)
- **Jack Ham**, LB (1971–82)
- **Franco Harris**, RB (1972–83)
- **Jack Lambert**, MLB (1974–84)
- **Troy Polamalu**, S (2003–14)
- **Ben Roethlisberger**, QB (2004–)
- **John Stallworth**, WR (1974–87)
- **Mike Webster**, C (1974–88)
- **Rod Woodson**, DB (1987–96)

COMBINING TEAMS

Many of the young men who played in the NFL were called to duty in World War II (1939–1945). In 1943, the Steelers and the Philadelphia Eagles did not have enough players on their own. They agreed to play the season as the Phil-Pitt Steagles. They shared coaches and players. They split time between the two cities. The combined team posted a 5–4–1 record.

In 1944, the Eagles were ready to go back on their own. The Steelers combined with the Chicago Cardinals. The second arrangement did not work nearly as well. The Chi/Pitt Cards/Steelers went 0–10.

JuJu Smith-Schuster, *left*, had just turned 22 when he was voted to the Pro Bowl in 2018.

TEAM STATS AND RECORDS

ALL-TIME RECORD

- **Regular Season:** 643–556–21
- **Postseason:** 36–26
- **Super Bowl Record:** 6–2

TOP COACHES

- **Chuck Noll** (1969–91); 193–148–1 (regular season); 16–8, 4 Super Bowl titles (postseason)
- **Bill Cowher** (1992–2006); 149–90–1 (regular season); 12–9, 1 Super Bowl title (postseason)
- **Mike Tomlin** (2007–); 145–78–1 (regular season); 8–8, 1 Super Bowl title (postseason)

CAREER OFFENSIVE LEADERS

- **Games played:** Ben Roethlisberger, 233
- **Passing yards:** Ben Roethlisberger, 60,348
- **Passing TDs:** Ben Roethlisberger, 396
- **Rushing yards:** Franco Harris, 11,950
- **Rushing TDs:** Franco Harris, 91
- **Receiving yards:** Hines Ward, 12,083
- **Receiving TDs:** Hines Ward, 85

CAREER DEFENSIVE LEADERS

- **Games played:** Donnie Shell, 201
- **Sacks:** James Harrison, 80.5
- **Tackles:** James Farrior, 740
- **Interceptions:** Mel Blount, 57
- **Fumble recoveries:** Ernie Stautner, 23

CAREER SPECIAL TEAMS LEADERS

- **Yards per punt:** Bobby Joe Green, 45.7
- **Field goals:** Gary Anderson, 309
- **Field goal percentage:** Chris Boswell, 88.0

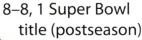
Ben Roethlisberger led the Steelers to two Super Bowl victories.

Terry Bradshaw rolls out to pass against the Rams in Super Bowl XIV. The Steelers won 31–19.

GREATEST SEASONS

The Steelers dynasty of the 1970s was one of the greatest in NFL history. They began their run by putting together a great defense known as the Steel Curtain. Defensive tackle Joe Greene, linebackers Jack Lambert and Jack Ham, cornerback Mel Blount, and safety Donnie Shell went on to the Pro Football Hall of Fame. Meanwhile, the offense featured Hall of Famers in quarterback Terry Bradshaw, running back Franco Harris, wide receivers Lynn Swann and John Stallworth, and center Mike Webster.

SAN FRANCISCO 49ERS

TEAM HISTORY

The 49ers started in the AAFC in 1946. They were one of three teams invited to join the NFL when the AAFC merged with the league after four seasons. For years the San Francisco 49ers were second best to their in-state rivals, the Los Angeles Rams. But that all changed in the 1980s. Head coach Bill Walsh built a team centered on an efficient passing game and a solid defense. Quarterback Joe Montana and the 49ers won four Super Bowls in the 1980s. Quarterback Steve Young led the 1994 team to a fifth title. The 49ers won more games than any other NFL team in the 1980s. Then they did it again in the 1990s. The 1994 team was the last to win a Super Bowl through 2020.

Jimmy Garoppolo arrived in 2017 to take over the Niners' starting quarterback job.

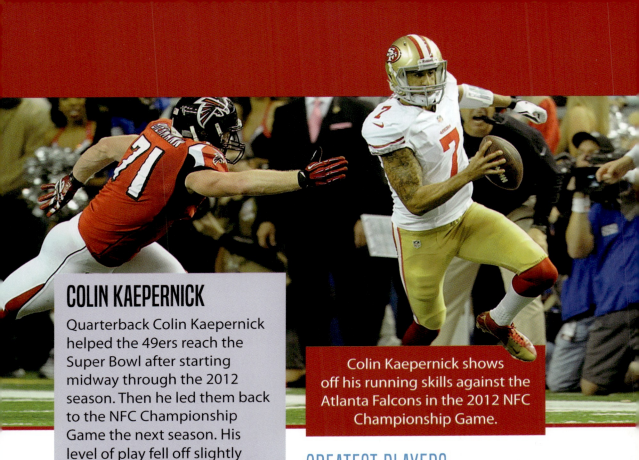

COLIN KAEPERNICK

Quarterback Colin Kaepernick helped the 49ers reach the Super Bowl after starting midway through the 2012 season. Then he led them back to the NFC Championship Game the next season. His level of play fell off slightly following those two successful seasons. In 2016, Kaepernick made headlines for a different reason. He took a knee during the national anthem. He was protesting police brutality throughout the country. It was one of the most controversial stories in the news for months. No NFL team signed him when his 49ers contract ended after the 2016 season. However, Kaepernick had plenty of support. He raised millions of dollars and donated it to charities.

Colin Kaepernick shows off his running skills against the Atlanta Falcons in the 2012 NFC Championship Game.

GREATEST PLAYERS

- **Dwight Clark**, WR (1979–87)
- **Roger Craig**, RB (1983–90)
- **Fred Dean**, DE (1981–85)
- **Frank Gore**, RB (2005–14)
- **Ronnie Lott**, DB (1981–90)
- **Joe Montana**, QB (1979–92)
- **Terrell Owens**, WR (1996–2003)
- **Joe Perry**, RB (1948–60, 1963)
- **Jerry Rice**, WR (1985–2000)
- **Y. A. Tittle**, QB (1951–60)
- **Patrick Willis**, LB (2007–14)
- **Steve Young**, QB (1987–99)

TEAM STATS AND RECORDS

ALL-TIME RECORD

- **Regular Season:** 589–499–16
- **Postseason:** 33–22
- **Super Bowl Record:** 5–2

TOP COACHES

- **Bill Walsh** (1979–88); 92–59–1 (regular season); 10–4, 3 Super Bowl titles (postseason)
- **George Seifert** (1989–96); 98–30 (regular season); 10–5, 2 Super Bowl titles (postseason)

CAREER OFFENSIVE LEADERS

- **Games played:** Jerry Rice, 238
- **Passing yards:** Joe Montana, 35,124
- **Passing TDs:** Joe Montana, 244
- **Rushing yards:** Frank Gore, 11,073
- **Rushing TDs:** Joe Perry, 68
- **Receiving yards:** Jerry Rice, 19,247
- **Receiving TDs:** Jerry Rice, 176

CAREER DEFENSIVE LEADERS

- **Games played:** Jimmy Johnson, 213
- **Sacks:** Bryant Young, 89.5
- **Tackles:** Patrick Willis, 733
- **Interceptions:** Ronnie Lott, 51
- **Fumble recoveries:** Kermit Alexander, 23

CAREER SPECIAL TEAMS LEADERS

- **Yards per punt:** Andy Lee, 46.2
- **Field goals:** Ray Wersching, 190
- **Field goal percentage:** Robbie Gould, 88.4

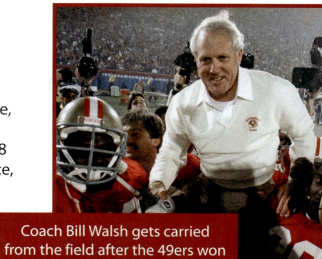

Coach Bill Walsh gets carried from the field after the 49ers won the Super Bowl in January 1985.

Hall of Famers Joe Perry (34) and Leo Nomellini (73) take the field before a game in the 1950s.

GREATEST SEASONS

The 49ers went a combined 10–38 between 1978 and 1980. Walsh quietly put together the pieces he needed to build a great team. Montana and wide receiver Dwight Clark arrived in 1979. Defensive backs Ronnie Lott and Eric Wright joined the team in 1981. Running back Roger Craig was drafted in 1983. Wide receiver Jerry Rice came aboard in 1985. They won Super Bowls after the 1981 and 1984 seasons. Then they went back-to-back in the 1988 and 1989 seasons.

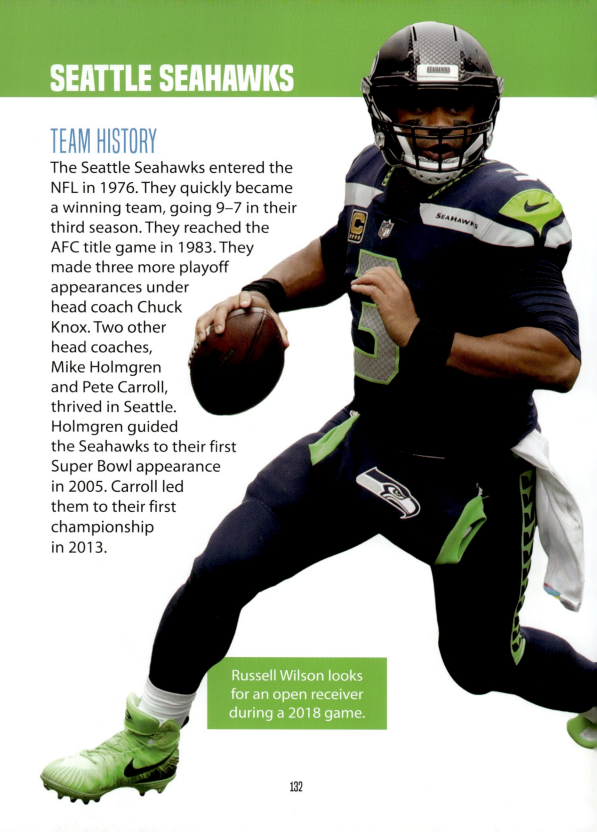

SEATTLE SEAHAWKS

TEAM HISTORY

The Seattle Seahawks entered the NFL in 1976. They quickly became a winning team, going 9–7 in their third season. They reached the AFC title game in 1983. They made three more playoff appearances under head coach Chuck Knox. Two other head coaches, Mike Holmgren and Pete Carroll, thrived in Seattle. Holmgren guided the Seahawks to their first Super Bowl appearance in 2005. Carroll led them to their first championship in 2013.

Russell Wilson looks for an open receiver during a 2018 game.

GREATEST PLAYERS

- **Shaun Alexander**, RB (2000–07)
- **Kenny Easley**, S (1981–87)
- **Jacob Green**, DE (1980–91)
- **Matt Hasselbeck**, QB (2001–10)
- **Walter Jones**, OT (1997–2008)
- **Cortez Kennedy**, DT (1990–2000)
- **Dave Krieg**, QB (1980–91)
- **Steve Largent**, WR (1976–89)
- **Marshawn Lynch**, RB (2010–15, 2019)
- **Richard Sherman**, DB (2011–17)
- **Russell Wilson**, QB (2012–)
- **Jim Zorn**, QB (1976–84)

MARSHAWN LYNCH

Marshawn Lynch joined the Seahawks in 2010. He earned the nickname "Beast Mode" for his aggressive running style. He displayed this in the 2010 playoffs against New Orleans. He helped clinch the game when he ran over, around, and through nearly the entire Saints defense on a 67-yard touchdown. The play had fans so excited that a nearby earthquake sensor registered a small tremor at the stadium.

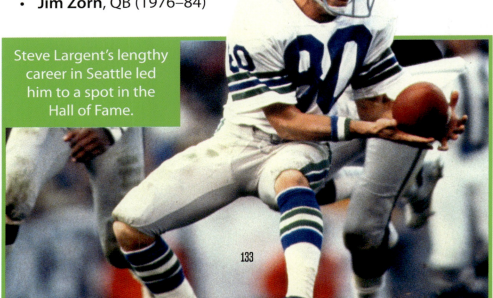

Steve Largent's lengthy career in Seattle led him to a spot in the Hall of Fame.

133

TEAM STATS AND RECORDS

ALL-TIME RECORD

- **Regular Season**: 367–340–1
- **Postseason**: 17–18
- **Super Bowl Record**: 1–2

TOP COACHES

- **Mike Holmgren** (1999–2008); 86–74 (regular season); 4–6 (postseason)
- **Pete Carroll** (2010–); 124–67–1 (regular season); 10–8, 1 Super Bowl title (postseason)

CAREER OFFENSIVE LEADERS

- **Games played**: Mack Strong, 201
- **Passing yards**: Russell Wilson, 33,946
- **Passing TDs**: Russell Wilson, 267
- **Rushing yards**: Shaun Alexander, 9,429
- **Rushing TDs**: Shaun Alexander, 100
- **Receiving yards**: Steve Largent, 13,089
- **Receiving TDs**: Steve Largent, 100

CAREER DEFENSIVE LEADERS

- **Games played**: Joe Nash, 218
- **Sacks**: Jacob Green, 97.5
- **Tackles**: Eugene Robinson, 942
- **Interceptions**: Dave Brown, 50
- **Fumble recoveries**: Jacob Green, 17

CAREER SPECIAL TEAMS LEADERS

- **Yards per punt**: Michael Dickson, 47.5
- **Field goals**: Stephen Hauschka, 175
- **Field goal percentage**: Jason Myers, 90.4

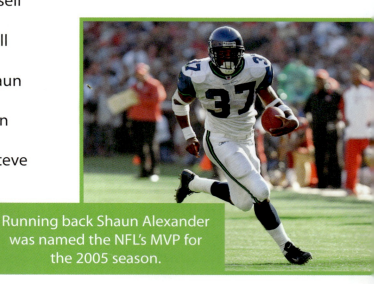

Running back Shaun Alexander was named the NFL's MVP for the 2005 season.

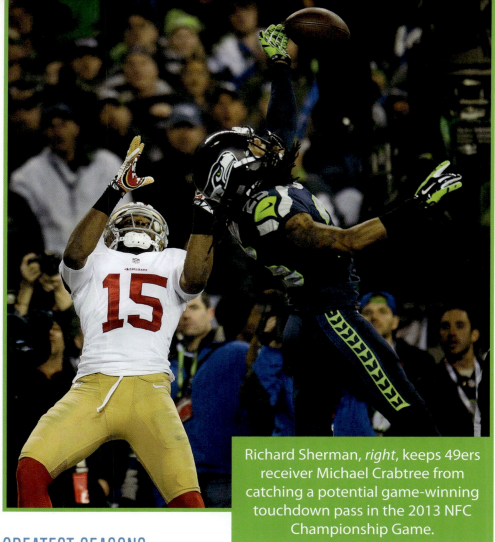

Richard Sherman, *right*, keeps 49ers receiver Michael Crabtree from catching a potential game-winning touchdown pass in the 2013 NFC Championship Game.

GREATEST SEASONS

In 2013, the Seahawks tied a team record with 13 victories. They lost only one game at home all year, as the loud crowds helped support the team. The defense was ranked No. 1 in the NFL. This was thanks in large part to defensive backs Richard Sherman, Earl Thomas, and Kam Chancellor. The secondary led the league with 28 interceptions. Quarterback Russell Wilson and running back Marshawn Lynch were the motor in the Seattle offense. They clinched the top seed in the NFC playoffs. The team won two close playoff games against the Saints and 49ers. Then the Seahawks blew out the Denver Broncos 43–8 to win Seattle's first Super Bowl title.

TAMPA BAY BUCCANEERS

TEAM HISTORY

The Buccaneers were a bit of a laughingstock when they joined the NFL in 1976. They lost all 14 games in their first season. The next year they started 0–12 before winning their final two games. But their rise to success was fast. Head coach John McKay and quarterback Doug Williams helped bring the Bucs to the 1979 NFC Championship Game. They made the playoffs again in 1981 and 1982, but more lean years followed. In 1996, head coach Tony Dungy brought the team back to life. The Buccaneers made the playoffs five times in six years. That included a Super Bowl victory in new coach Jon Gruden's first season. They did it again in 2020 after Tom Brady arrived from New England to quarterback the team.

TAMPA 2

Tampa Bay earned a reputation for strong defense in the late 1990s. The Bucs ranked in the top three in total defense from 1997 to 1999. They frequently used a Cover 2 defensive system. The system uses two safeties to cover the deep zones away from the ball. Cornerbacks and linebackers cover the rest. With fast athletes, it can be effective. The Bucs played it so well that it came to be known as the "Tampa 2."

GREATEST PLAYERS

- **Mike Alstott**, FB (1996–2006)
- **Ronde Barber**, CB (1997–2012)
- **Tom Brady**, QB (2020–)
- **Derrick Brooks**, LB (1995–2008)
- **Mike Evans**, WR (2014–)
- **Jimmie Giles**, TE (1978–86)
- **John Lynch**, S (1993–2003)
- **Hardy Nickerson**, LB (1993–99)
- **Warren Sapp**, DT (1995–2003)
- **Lee Roy Selmon**, DE (1976–84)
- **James Wilder**, RB (1981–89)
- **Doug Williams**, QB (1978–82)

Quarterback Tom Brady drops back for a handoff during a 2021 game.

TEAM STATS AND RECORDS

ALL-TIME RECORD

- **Regular Season**: 278–429–1
- **Postseason**: 10–9
- **Super Bowl Record**: 2–0

TOP COACHES

- **Tony Dungy** (1996–2001); 54–42 (regular season); 2–4 (postseason)
- **Jon Gruden** (2002–08); 57–55 (regular season); 3–2, 1 Super Bowl title (postseason)

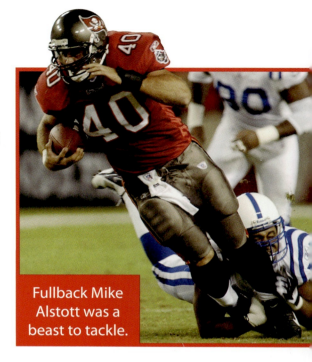

Fullback Mike Alstott was a beast to tackle.

CAREER OFFENSIVE LEADERS

- **Games played**: Dave Moore, 190
- **Passing yards**: Jameis Winston, 19,737
- **Passing TDs**: Jameis Winston, 121
- **Rushing yards**: James Wilder, 5,957
- **Rushing TDs**: Mike Alstott, 58
- **Receiving yards**: Mike Evans, 8,266
- **Receiving TDs**: Mike Evans, 61

CAREER DEFENSIVE LEADERS

- **Games played**: Ronde Barber, 241
- **Sacks**: Warren Sapp, 77
- **Tackles**: Derrick Brooks, 1,300
- **Interceptions**: Ronde Barber, 47
- **Fumble recoveries**: Lavonte David, 16

CAREER SPECIAL TEAMS LEADERS

- **Yards per punt**: Bryan Anger, 45.0
- **Field goals**: Martin Gramatica, 137
- **Field goal percentage**: Connor Barth, 83.8

GREATEST SEASONS

Dungy's Buccaneers reached the playoffs four times in six years. However, they didn't have much success there. In 2002, the team brought in former Raiders head coach Jon Gruden to take the reins. He led the Bucs to a franchise-record 12 wins on the back of a strong defense. That defense featured future Hall of Famers Warren Sapp on the defensive line, Derrick Brooks at linebacker, and John Lynch at safety. After two comfortable playoff victories, the Bucs faced the Raiders in the Super Bowl. The defense made five interceptions. It returned three of them for touchdowns. The final score was 48–21, giving the Bucs their first NFL title.

The Buccaneers' Warren Sapp kisses the Vince Lombardi Trophy after Tampa Bay won its first Super Bowl.

TENNESSEE TITANS

Running back Derrick Henry runs the ball past the Ravens in a 2021 game.

TEAM HISTORY

The Houston Oilers were one of the original eight teams in the AFL. They won the first two AFL titles. They reached the playoffs three more times before the league merged with the NFL in 1970. The Oilers had a number of exciting players and high-scoring teams over the years. But they didn't reach the Super Bowl until after team owner Bud Adams moved them in 1997. They became the first major pro sports team to call Nashville, Tennessee, their

A NEW NAME

At first, the Tennessee Oilers struggled to connect with fans in their new home. Owner Bud Adams thought giving the team a new name would help. In 1998, he put together a group of experts on Tennessee. They chose Titans for a nickname. Adams wanted a name that showed strength and heroism. In addition, Nashville's nickname is "Athens of the South." Athens is the capital of Greece. The Titans were creatures from Greek mythology.

home. Head coach Jeff Fisher took them to the Super Bowl after the 1999 season. They've had some great teams since. However, through 2020 they were still looking to get back to the big game.

GREATEST PLAYERS

- **Elvin Bethea**, DE (1968–83)
- **Earl Campbell**, RB (1978–84)
- **Ray Childress**, DL (1985–95)
- **Eddie George**, RB (1996–2003)
- **Ernest Givins**, WR (1986–94)
- **Charley Hennigan**, WR (1960–66)
- **Derrick Henry**, RB (2016–)
- **Ken Houston**, S (1967–72)
- **Bruce Matthews**, OL (1983–2001)
- **Steve McNair**, QB (1995–2005)
- **Warren Moon**, QB (1984–93)
- **Dan Pastorini**, QB (1971–79)

It usually took more than one defender to bring down Earl Campbell.

141

TEAM STATS AND RECORDS

ALL-TIME RECORD

- **Regular Season**: 451–475–6
- **Postseason**: 17–22
- **Super Bowl Record**: 0–1

TOP COACHES

- **Bum Phillips** (1975–80); 55–35 (regular season); 4–3 (postseason)
- **Jeff Fisher** (1994–2020); 142–120 (regular season); 5–6 (postseason)

CAREER OFFENSIVE LEADERS

- **Games played**: Bruce Matthews, 296
- **Passing yards**: Warren Moon, 33,685
- **Passing TDs**: Warren Moon, 196
- **Rushing yards**: Eddie George, 10,009
- **Rushing TDs**: Earl Campbell, 73
- **Receiving yards**: Ernest Givins, 7,935
- **Receiving TDs**: Charley Hennigan, 51

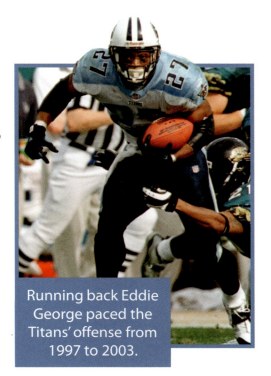

Running back Eddie George paced the Titans' offense from 1997 to 2003.

CAREER DEFENSIVE LEADERS

- **Games played**: Elvin Bethea, 210
- **Sacks**: Ray Childress, 75.5
- **Tackles**: Ray Childress, 858
- **Interceptions**: Jim Norton, 45
- **Fumble recoveries**: Ray Childress, 19

CAREER SPECIAL TEAMS LEADERS

- **Yards per punt**: Brett Kern, 45.9
- **Field goals**: Al Del Greco, 246
- **Field goal percentage**: Rob Bironas, 85.7

GREATEST SEASONS

After playing two seasons as the Tennessee Oilers, the team got a makeover in 1999. They received new uniforms and a new nickname, the Titans. The team got off to a 6–1 start. Quarterback Steve McNair, running back Eddie George, and defensive end Jevon Kearse led the way to a 13–3 record and a wild-card berth. In their first playoff game, they were saved by a miracle. It was a trick play on a last-second kickoff return that gave the Titans a win over Buffalo. They rode that momentum to wins at Indianapolis and Jacksonville. But they came up just short in the Super Bowl against the St. Louis Rams. Receiver Kevin Dyson was tackled at the 1-yard line on the final play of a 23–16 defeat.

Kevin Dyson's trick play touchdown against Buffalo became known as the "Music City Miracle."

TEAM HISTORY

Washington joined the NFL in 1932. They were called the Boston Braves. After one year, the team changed its name to the Redskins. In 1937, owner George Preston Marshall moved the team to Washington, DC.

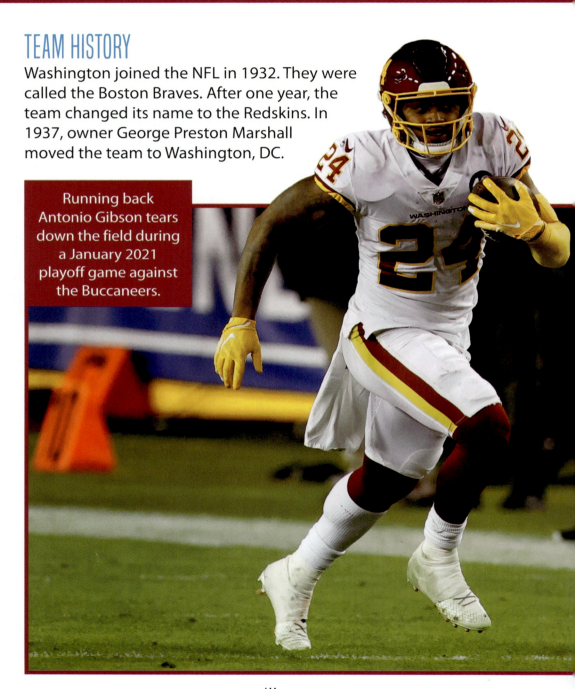

Running back Antonio Gibson tears down the field during a January 2021 playoff game against the Buccaneers.

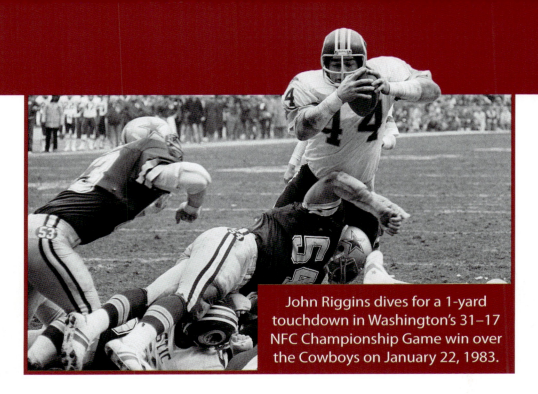

John Riggins dives for a 1-yard touchdown in Washington's 31–17 NFC Championship Game win over the Cowboys on January 22, 1983.

The team itself was beloved by football fans in the nation's capital. However, over the years it became clear that a new nickname was needed. The term *redskin* is a slur used to mock Indigenous peoples. In 2020, the old nickname was dropped. The team was officially called the Washington Football Team while the organization worked to pick a new nickname.

GREATEST PLAYERS

- **Sammy Baugh**, QB-DB-P (1937–52)
- **Darrell Green**, CB (1983–2002)
- **Russ Grimm**, G (1981–91)
- **Sonny Jurgensen**, QB (1964–74)
- **Billy Kilmer**, QB (1971–78)
- **Bobby Mitchell**, RB-WR (1962–68)

- **Art Monk**, WR (1980–93)
- **John Riggins**, RB (1976–79, 1981–85)
- **Mark Rypien**, QB (1988–93)
- **Charley Taylor**, RB-WR (1964–75, 1977)
- **Joe Theismann**, QB (1974–85)
- **Doug Williams**, QB (1986–89)

TEAM STATS AND RECORDS

ALL-TIME RECORD
- **Regular Season:** 610–612–28
- **Postseason:** 23–20
- **Super Bowl Record:** 3–2

TOP COACHES
- **George Allen** (1971–77); 67–30–1 (regular season); 2–5 (postseason)
- **Joe Gibbs** (1981–92, 2004–07); 154–94 (regular season); 17–7, 3 Super Bowl titles (postseason)

CAREER OFFENSIVE LEADERS
- **Games played:** Art Monk, 205
- **Passing yards:** Joe Theismann, 25,206
- **Passing TDs:** Sammy Baugh, 187
- **Rushing yards:** John Riggins, 7,472
- **Rushing TDs:** John Riggins, 79
- **Receiving yards:** Art Monk, 12,026
- **Receiving TDs:** Charley Taylor, 79

CAREER DEFENSIVE LEADERS
- **Games played:** Darrell Green, 295
- **Sacks:** Ryan Kerrigan, 95.5
- **Tackles:** Darrell Green, 1,162
- **Interceptions:** Darrell Green, 54
- **Fumble recoveries:** Chris Hanburger, 17

CAREER SPECIAL TEAMS LEADERS
- **Yards per punt:** Tress Way, 46.8
- **Field goals:** Mark Moseley, 263
- **Field goal percentage:** Kai Forbath, 87.0

GREATEST SEASONS

The 1982 NFL season was interrupted by a players' strike. Washington was 2–0 when players walked off the job. When they returned in November, they won six of their final seven games to post a league-best 8–1 record. Washington won three straight playoff games to reach the Super Bowl. Trailing the Miami Dolphins early in the fourth quarter, fullback John Riggins broke free for a 43-yard touchdown run to put Washington ahead. Joe Theismann later threw his second touchdown pass of the game to get a 27–17 victory and Washington's first Super Bowl title.

THE HOGS

"The Hogs" was the nickname for Washington's big, strong offensive linemen and tight ends. They dominated opposing defenses in the 1980s and 1990s. They formed the foundation for the three NFL championship teams.

Quarterback Joe Theismann scrambles out of the pocket during Super Bowl XVII.

LANCE ALWORTH WR

San Diego Chargers (1962–70), Dallas Cowboys (1971–72)

Lance Alworth led the league in receptions, receiving yards, and touchdown catches three times each. Alworth was the AFL Player of the Year in 1963, when he was the top receiver for the Chargers. In 1972 he caught a touchdown pass to help the Cowboys win Super Bowl VI.

Games: 136
Receptions: 542
Receiving yards: 10,266
Receiving touchdowns: 85
Awards: AFL Player of the Year (1963), seven AFL All-Star Games, six First Team All-AFL

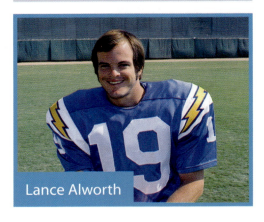

Lance Alworth

CHAMP BAILEY CB

Washington Redskins (1999–2003), Denver Broncos (2004–13)

Champ Bailey was one of the top cornerbacks of his generation. Bailey led the NFL with ten interceptions in 2006. He retired as the NFL's career leader in passes defended—a statistic that wasn't tracked until 1999. He might be best remembered for intercepting New England's Tom Brady in the end zone and returning it 100 yards during a January 2006 playoff game. That interception helped the Broncos defeat the two-time defending champion Patriots 27–13.

Games: 215
Interceptions: 52
Tackles: 931
Sacks: 3
Touchdowns: 5
Awards: 12 Pro Bowls, three First Team All-Pro

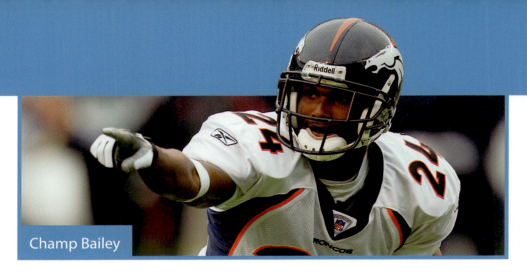

Champ Bailey

MEL BLOUNT CB
Pittsburgh Steelers (1970–83)

Mel Blount was a physical cornerback. He used his size to overpower smaller receivers and his speed to keep up with the faster ones. Blount's coverage was a key part of Pittsburgh's Steel Curtain defense. It allowed the pass rushers extra time to get to the quarterback. He won four Super Bowls with the Steelers. In 1975, he was the NFL Defensive Player of the Year, leading the league with 11 interceptions.

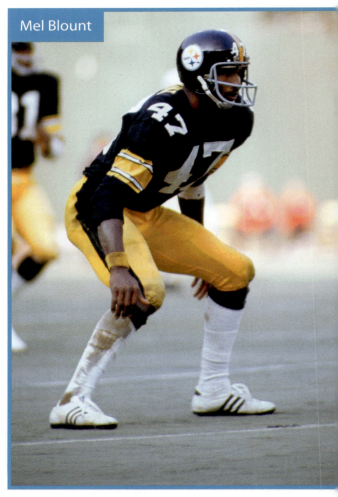

Mel Blount

Games: 200
Interceptions: 57
Touchdowns: 4
Awards: NFL Defensive Player of the Year (1975), five Pro Bowls, two First Team All-Pro

TOM BRADY QB

New England Patriots (2000–19), Tampa Bay Buccaneers (2020–)

Tom Brady was a sixth-round draft pick. He saw action in only one game as a rookie. But when Patriots starter Drew Bledsoe was injured early in the 2001 season, Brady stepped into the spotlight and never looked back. He led the Patriots to three Super Bowl victories in his first four years as a starter. He won three more titles during his 20 years in New England. In 2020, he signed with the Buccaneers as a free agent and immediately led Tampa Bay to a Super Bowl victory, his seventh. No other quarterback has started and won more than four Super Bowls.

Tom Brady

Games: 301
Passing yards: 79,204
Passing touchdowns: 581
Rushing yards: 1,043
Rushing touchdowns: 25
Awards: Super Bowl MVP (2001, 2003, 2014, 2016, 2020), NFL MVP (2007, 2010, 2017), NFL Offensive Player of the Year (2007, 2010), 14 Pro Bowls, three First Team All-Pro

DREW BREES QB

San Diego Chargers (2001–05),
New Orleans Saints (2006–20)

Drew Brees was often overlooked due to his size. Despite standing just over 6 feet tall, he put together one of the greatest careers of any quarterback in NFL history. He never had the strongest arm, but his pinpoint accuracy more than made up for it. Brees was remarkably durable as well. He missed only two games in his first 12 seasons with the Saints. He retired in 2020 as the NFL's career leader in completions and passing yards. His streak of 54 games with at least one touchdown pass is the longest of all time.

Games: 287
Passing yards: 80,358
Passing touchdowns: 571
Rushing yards: 752
Rushing touchdowns: 25
Awards: Super Bowl MVP (2009), NFL Offensive Player of the Year (2008, 2011), 13 Pro Bowls, one First Team All-Pro

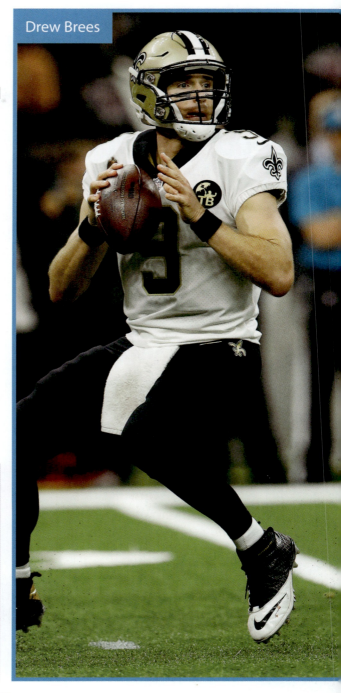

Drew Brees

Derrick Brooks

DERRICK BROOKS LB

Tampa Bay Buccaneers (1995–2008)

Games: 224
Tackles: 1,713
Sacks: 13.5
Interceptions: 25
Fumble recoveries: 4
Touchdowns: 7
Awards: NFL Defensive Player of the Year (2002), 11 Pro Bowls, five First Team All-Pro

Derrick Brooks was an elite tackler with the speed to handle tight ends and running backs in pass coverage. He led the league in solo tackles three times and also had a nose for the end zone. In 2002, he intercepted five passes and returned three of them for touchdowns. He also scored during the Super Bowl that season, helping lift the Bucs past the Raiders.

JIM BROWN RB

Cleveland Browns (1957–65)

Games: 118
Rushing yards: 12,312
Rushing touchdowns: 106
Receptions: 262
Receiving yards: 2,499
Receiving touchdowns: 20
Awards: NFL MVP (1957–58, 1963, 1965), NFL Offensive Rookie of the Year (1957), nine Pro Bowls, eight First Team All-Pro

Jim Brown held the unofficial title of "Greatest Running Back in NFL History" for years. Some might argue he still does. No player can match most of his accomplishments. In nine NFL seasons, Brown led the league in rushing yards eight times and in rushing touchdowns five times. Brown had the size of many fullbacks but the speed and agility of a tailback. He became the first NFL player to score 100 career touchdowns. He held the career rushing mark until 1984, when he was passed by Walter Payton.

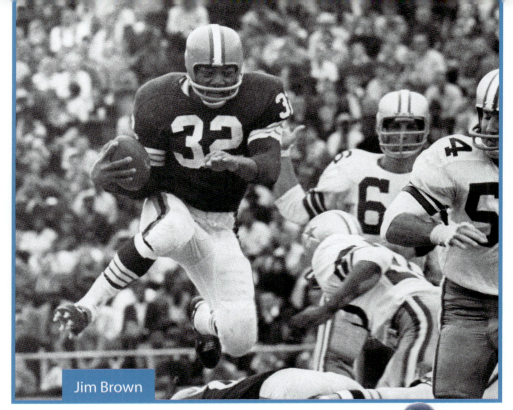
Jim Brown

DICK BUTKUS LB
Chicago Bears (1965–73)

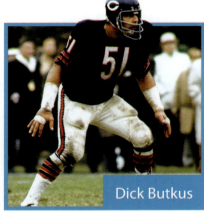
Dick Butkus

Dick Butkus is from Chicago. He joined the Bears as the third overall pick in the 1965 draft. He immediately went to work making the lives of opposing ballcarriers miserable. Butkus relied on his quickness and instinct to fill running lanes. He used his strength and toughness to make bone-shaking tackles. He missed only two games in his first eight years, but a lingering knee injury forced his early retirement in 1973. Since 1985, the top college linebacker of the year has received the Butkus Award.

Games: 119
Interceptions: 22
Fumble recoveries: 27
Touchdowns: 1
Awards: Eight Pro Bowls, five First Team All-Pro

AARON DONALD DL

St. Louis Rams (2014–15), Los Angeles Rams (2016–)

A Pro Bowl player in each of his first seven NFL seasons, Aaron Donald was the 14th pick in the 2014 draft. He quickly became a feared pass rusher and run stopper for the Rams. He posted double-digit quarterback sacks in five of his first seven seasons. His career-high total of 20.5 sacks led the NFL in 2018. Two seasons later he was up to 85.5 total sacks.

Games: 110
Tackles: 357
Sacks: 85.5
Forced fumbles: 19
Fumble recoveries: 6
Awards: NFL Defensive Player of the Year (2017–18, 2020), NFL Defensive Rookie of the Year (2014), seven Pro Bowls, six First Team All-Pro

Aaron Donald

LARRY FITZGERALD WR

Arizona Cardinals (2004–20)

The third pick of the 2004 NFL Draft, Larry Fitzgerald emerged as a star in his second season when he led the league with 103 receptions at age 22. He did it again with 107 catches in 2016, when he was 33. Fitzgerald also led the NFL in touchdown receptions twice.

Larry Fitzgerald

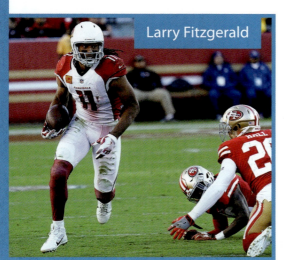

Games: 263
Receptions: 1,432
Receiving yards: 17,492
Receiving touchdowns: 121
Awards: 11 Pro Bowls, one First Team All-Pro

Tony Gonzalez

TONY GONZALEZ TE

Kansas City Chiefs (1997–2008), Atlanta Falcons (2009–13)

Through 2020, Tony Gonzalez ranked third on the NFL's career receptions list, a remarkable feat for a tight end. But he was no ordinary athlete. Gonzalez also played basketball in college, and he used his elite athletic ability to revolutionize the tight end position. He used his quickness and body control to get open and make catches. Then his speed allowed him to add yards after the catch. Gonzalez ranks sixth on the all-time receiving yards list and has 2,000 more than any other tight end.

Games: 270
Receptions: 1,325
Receiving yards: 15,127
Receiving touchdowns: 111
Awards: 14 Pro Bowls, six First Team All-Pro

OTTO GRAHAM QB
Cleveland Browns (1946–55)

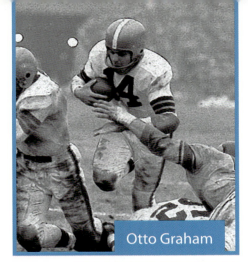

Otto Graham

Otto Graham had a remarkable career. He led the Browns to four straight AAFC championships. Then the Browns joined the NFL in 1950. Graham quarterbacked them to the NFL Championship Game in each of their first six seasons, winning three more titles. Graham was named his league's MVP multiple times. He was known for his instincts and a soft touch on his passes.

Games: 126
Passing yards: 23,584
Passing touchdowns: 174
Rushing yards: 405
Rushing touchdowns: 44
Awards: NFL MVP (1951, 1953, 1955), five Pro Bowls, seven First Team All-Pro

DARRELL GREEN CB
Washington Redskins (1983–2002)

Games: 295
Interceptions: 54
Tackles: 1,202
Touchdowns: 8
Awards: Seven Pro Bowls, one First Team All-Pro

Darrell Green used his sprinter's speed to shut down opposing wide receivers. He earned the nickname the "Ageless Wonder" by maintaining his level of play long past the point when most cornerbacks retire. He started all 16 games at age 39, and he stayed on as a part-time player for three seasons after that.

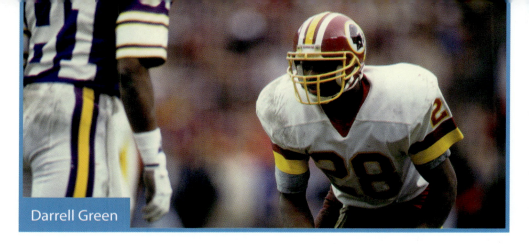
Darrell Green

JOE GREENE DT
Pittsburgh Steelers (1969–81)

Joe Greene was widely considered the most dominant defensive lineman of the 1970s. He was the focal point of Pittsburgh's Steel Curtain defense and helped the team win four Super Bowls in a six-year span. His quickness allowed him to fly past opposing linemen and get to the quarterback. Although he was an intimidating presence on the field, Green had a reputation as a nice guy off it.

Games: 181
Fumble recoveries: 16
Awards: NFL Defensive Player of the Year (1972, 1974), NFL Defensive Rookie of the Year (1969), ten Pro Bowls, four First Team All-Pro

Joe Greene

JOHN HANNAH G

New England Patriots (1973–85)

John Hannah was featured on the cover of a 1981 issue of *Sports Illustrated* accompanied by a headline that read, "The Best Offensive Lineman of All Time." In 1978, the Patriots rushed for an NFL record of 3,165 yards behind an offensive line anchored by Hannah. He was later named as one of three guards on the NFL's 75th Anniversary All-Time Team.

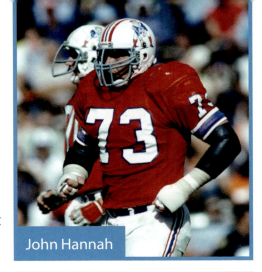
John Hannah

Games: 183
Fumble recoveries: 10
Awards: Nine Pro Bowls, seven First Team All-Pro

DON HUTSON WR

Green Bay Packers (1935–45)

Don Hutson was a talented safety who led the NFL in interceptions in 1940. He served as the Packers' placekicker for the latter half of his career. But he is best known as the first modern wide receiver. Hutson was credited with inventing a number of pass routes that remain popular today. He used those routes and his soft hands to rewrite the NFL record books.

Don Hutson

Games: 116
Receptions: 488
Receiving yards: 7,991
Receiving touchdowns: 99
Awards: NFL MVP (1941–42), four Pro Bowls, eight First Team All-Pro

DEACON JONES DE

Los Angeles Rams (1961–71),
San Diego Chargers (1972–73),
Washington Redskins (1974)

David "Deacon" Jones was an expert at sacking quarterbacks. In fact, he's credited with coming up with the term *sack* for tackling the quarterback behind the line of scrimmage. With the Rams, Jones anchored the Fearsome Foursome, now considered one of the best defensive lines in NFL history. Though sacks weren't an official NFL statistic until 1982, he's unofficially credited with 173.5 career sacks. That would have been an NFL record at the time and would rank third on the all-time list today.

Games: 191
Fumble recoveries: 15
Awards: Eight Pro Bowls, five First Team All-Pro

Deacon Jones

JACK LAMBERT LB

Pittsburgh Steelers (1974–84)

Jack Lambert was a key figure in the Steel Curtain defense that helped Pittsburgh win four Super Bowls in six seasons. Their first title came in Lambert's rookie season, when he stepped into the starting lineup in Week 1 and stayed there all season. Lambert had the quickness to excel in pass coverage in addition to his bone-jarring tackling abilities. He also had a nose for the football, evidenced by his league-high eight fumble recoveries in 1976. That year he was also named NFL Defensive Player of the Year.

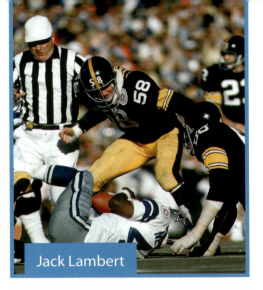

Jack Lambert

Games: 146
Interceptions: 28
Fumble recoveries: 17
Awards: NFL Defensive Player of the Year (1976), NFL Defensive Rookie of the Year (1974), nine Pro Bowls, six First Team All-Pro

DICK "NIGHT TRAIN" LANE CB

Los Angeles Rams (1952–53), Chicago Cardinals (1954–59), Detroit Lions (1960–65)

Dick Lane, nicknamed the "Night Train," earned a reputation during his rookie year as one of the most dangerous cornerbacks in the NFL. He intercepted 14 passes as a rookie, a mark that remained the NFL's single-season record through 2020. He also was a hard hitter who was one of the most feared tacklers in the game.

Games: 157
Interceptions: 68
Touchdowns: 8
Awards: Seven Pro Bowls, three First Team All-Pro

RAY LEWIS LB

Baltimore Ravens (1996–2012)

During his time with the Ravens, Ray Lewis assumed leadership of the defense. He led the NFL in tackles three times in his first six seasons. He retired as the league's leading tackler of all time. The 2000 Ravens defense set NFL records for fewest points and rushing yards allowed in a season. Lewis led that team to a Super Bowl victory and earned the game's MVP award. He went out on top in 2012, leading the Ravens to another Super Bowl run. Lewis averaged nearly 13 tackles per game during that postseason.

Games: 228
Tackles: 2,059
Sacks: 41.5
Interceptions: 31
Fumble recoveries: 20
Touchdowns: 3
Awards: Super Bowl MVP (2000), NFL Defensive Player of the Year (2000, 2003), 13 Pro Bowls, seven First Team All-Pro

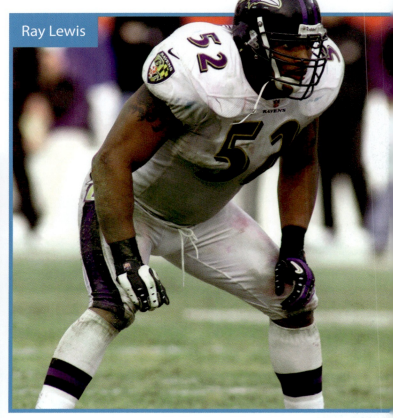

Ray Lewis

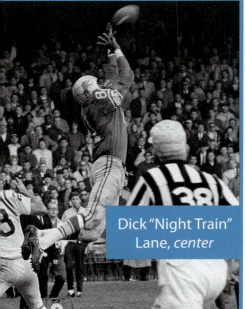

Dick "Night Train" Lane, *center*

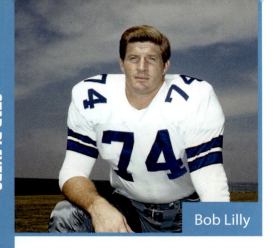
Bob Lilly

BOB LILLY DT
Dallas Cowboys (1961–74)

Bob Lilly missed just one game in his 14-year career. He was the first player to be inducted into the Cowboys' Ring of Honor. Lilly was a key part of the defense that helped the Cowboys win seven division titles in eight seasons. He also played a huge role in Dallas's Super Bowl VI victory. His 29-yard sack of Miami quarterback Bob Griese was the game's iconic play.

Games: 196
Fumble recoveries: 18
Interceptions: 1
Touchdowns: 4
Awards: 11 Pro Bowls, seven First Team All-Pro

RONNIE LOTT DB
San Francisco 49ers (1981–90), Los Angeles Raiders (1991–92), New York Jets (1993–94)

Ronnie Lott began his career at cornerback and picked off seven passes during his rookie season. In addition to being a dangerous ball hawk, Lott was one of the game's most effective tacklers. He also came up huge in big spots, with nine interceptions and two touchdowns in 20 career postseason games.

Games: 192
Interceptions: 63
Tackles: 1,146
Sacks: 8.5
Touchdowns: 5
Awards: Ten Pro Bowls, six First Team All-Pro

Ronnie Lott

PEYTON MANNING QB
Indianapolis Colts (1998–2010), Denver Broncos (2012–15)

Peyton Manning is a son of the longtime NFL quarterback Archie Manning. Peyton had big shoes to fill, but he did so admirably. As the first pick in the 1998 draft, Peyton took over as the Colts' starting quarterback. Along the way, he led the NFL in completions and touchdown passes three times. He guided the Colts to a Super Bowl victory after the 2006 season. The five-time NFL MVP ended his career with four seasons in Denver, where he broke the NFL record for passing yards in a season with 5,477 and led the Broncos to consecutive Super Bowls. He walked off the field a champion, winning his final game against the Panthers in the Super Bowl.

Games: 266
Passing yards: 71,940
Passing touchdowns: 539
Rushing yards: 667
Rushing touchdowns: 18
Awards: NFL MVP (2003–04, 2008–09, 2013), NFL Offensive Player of the Year (2004, 2013), Super Bowl MVP (2006), 14 Pro Bowls, seven First Team All-Pro

Peyton Manning

BRUCE MATTHEWS OL

Houston Oilers (1983–96), Tennessee Oilers (1997–98), Tennessee Titans (1999–2001)

Bruce Matthews was a versatile and durable lineman. He was a star in both Houston and Tennessee. He never missed a game due to injury, and he ranks fifth among non-kickers in career games played. Matthews is one of the rare players to start at least one game at every spot on the offensive line during his career. He also served as the team's long snapper. His 14 Pro Bowls are tied for the most in NFL history.

Games: 296
Fumble recoveries: 10
Awards: 14 Pro Bowls, seven First Team All-Pro

Bruce Matthews

JOE MONTANA QB

San Francisco 49ers (1974–90, 1992), Kansas City Chiefs (1993–94)

Joe Montana was more than just a three-time Super Bowl MVP. He was the master of the comeback. Including the playoffs, he engineered 31 fourth-quarter comeback victories. Two of his most famous came in the 1981 NFC Championship Game against Dallas and in Super Bowl XXIII against the Bengals. An effective scrambler early in his career, Montana suffered back injuries that held him back later. But he still led the NFL in completion percentage five times and was the face of the 49ers dynasty.

Games: 192
Passing yards: 40,551
Passing touchdowns: 273
Rushing yards: 1,676
Rushing touchdowns: 20
Awards: NFL MVP (1989–90), NFL Offensive Player of the Year (1989), Super Bowl MVP (1981, 1984, 1989), eight Pro Bowls, three First Team All-Pro

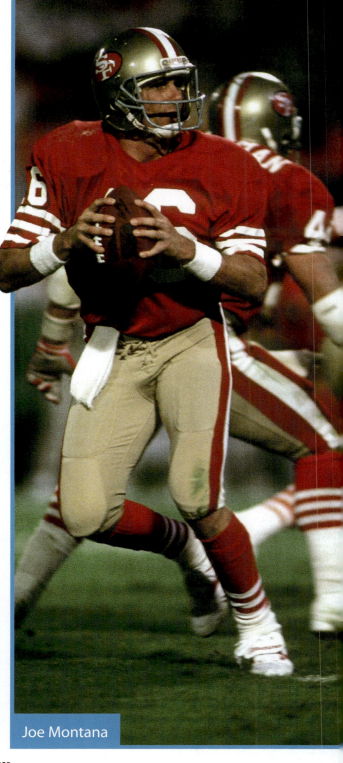
Joe Montana

RANDY MOSS WR

Minnesota Vikings (1998–2004, 2010), Oakland Raiders (2005–06), New England Patriots (2007–10), Tennessee Titans (2010), San Francisco 49ers (2012)

Games: 218
Receptions: 982
Receiving yards: 15,292
Receiving touchdowns: 156
Awards: NFL Offensive Rookie of the Year (1998), six Pro Bowls, four First Team All-Pro

Randy Moss burst onto the scene in 1998. He helped the Vikings to a 15–1 record with his dynamic play. He led the NFL in touchdown catches five times. His 23 scores in 2007 were a league record through 2020. Moss was so good that rivals crafted game plans around taking him out of the game.

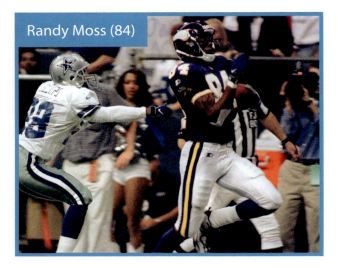
Randy Moss (84)

ANTHONY MUÑOZ T

Cincinnati Bengals (1980–92)

Games: 185
Fumble recoveries: 6
Touchdowns: 4
Awards: 11 Pro Bowls, nine First Team All-Pro

Anthony Muñoz worked as a left tackle for 13 seasons in Cincinnati. He played a key role in helping the Bengals reach the Super Bowl after the 1981 and 1989 seasons. Muñoz was a durable player. He started all but three games, which he missed due to injury, from 1980 to 1991. He was one of three tackles named to the NFL's 75th Anniversary All-Time Team.

Anthony Muñoz

JIM OTTO c

Oakland Raiders (1960–74)

Jim Otto was thought to be undersized for a center. But he proved to be as durable as he was effective. He played 210 consecutive games for the great Raiders teams of the 1960s and early 1970s. Wearing his trademark 00 jersey, Otto was the only player to start every game for the same team during all ten years of the AFL's existence.

Games: 210
Fumble recoveries: 3
Awards: Nine AFL All-Star games, three Pro Bowls, ten First Team All-Pro

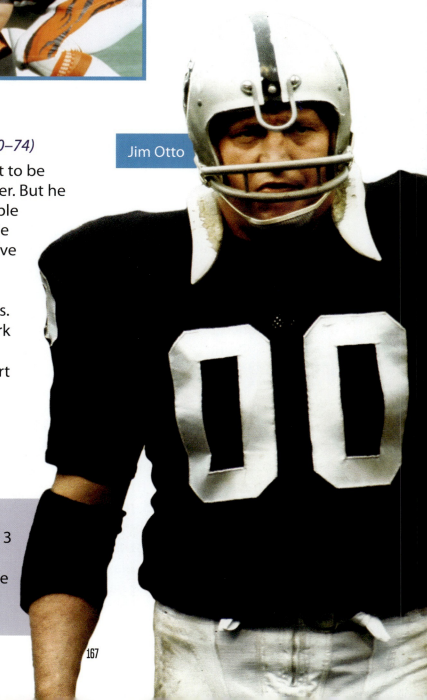

Jim Otto

ALAN PAGE DT

Minnesota Vikings (1967–78), Chicago Bears (1978–81)

A fearsome pass rusher who anchored Minnesota's famed Purple People Eaters, Alan Page was the first defensive player to win the NFL MVP Award. He weighed just 245 pounds at his peak, which is small for a defensive tackle. However, he thrived due to his quickness and intelligence.

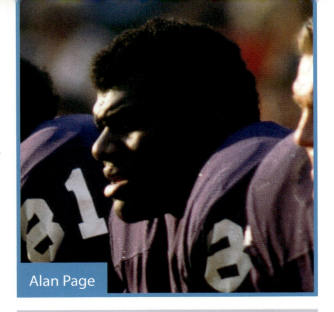

Alan Page

Games: 218
Fumble recoveries: 23
Interceptions: 2
Touchdowns: 1
Awards: NFL MVP (1971), NFL Defensive Player of the Year (1971), nine Pro Bowls, six First Team All-Pro

WALTER PAYTON RB

Chicago Bears (1975–87)

Walter Payton could push past or through any would-be tackler. He also used his leaping ability to soar over the line and into the end zone. In 1977, he set an NFL record (since broken) when he rushed for 275 yards in a game against the Vikings. When he retired, he was the NFL's career leader in rushing yards, touchdowns, and receptions by a running back.

Games: 190
Rushing yards: 16,726
Rushing touchdowns: 110
Receptions: 492
Receiving yards: 4,538
Receiving touchdowns: 15
Awards: NFL MVP (1977), NFL Offensive Player of the Year (1977), nine Pro Bowls, five First Team All-Pro

ADRIAN PETERSON RB

Minnesota Vikings (2007–16), New Orleans Saints (2017), Arizona Cardinals (2017), Washington Redskins (2018–19), Detroit Lions (2020)

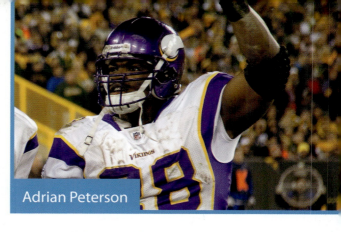

Adrian Peterson

A remarkable athlete with breakaway speed, Adrian Peterson threatened to go the distance any time he touched the ball. In just his eighth game as a pro, Peterson set the NFL's single-game rushing record when he ran for 296 yards against the Chargers. The next year he won the first of his three NFL rushing titles. His most remarkable season came in 2012. Just nine months after tearing his ACL, Peterson returned for Week 1 and didn't miss a beat. He rushed for 100 yards ten times that season, including 199 in the last game of the season. That victory put the Vikings into the playoffs. It also gave him 2,097 rushing yards that season. That's just 8 yards short of Eric Dickerson's NFL record.

Games: 180
Rushing yards: 14,820
Rushing touchdowns: 118
Receptions: 301
Receiving yards: 2,466
Receiving touchdowns: 6
Awards: NFL MVP (2012), NFL Offensive Rookie of the Year (2007), NFL Offensive Player of the Year (2012), seven Pro Bowls, four First Team All-Pro

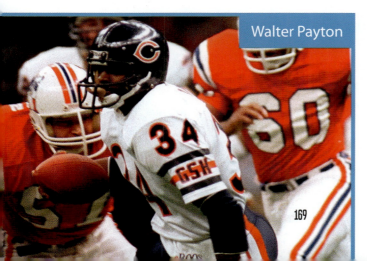

Walter Payton

169

JOHN RANDLE DT

Minnesota Vikings (1990–2000),
Seattle Seahawks (2001–03)

John Randle was viewed as too small to play in the NFL. He went undrafted coming out of college. Randle proved the scouts wrong by becoming one of the game's greatest defensive tackles. Unusually quick and always relentless in his pursuit of the quarterback, Randle led the NFL with a career-best 15.5 sacks in 1997.

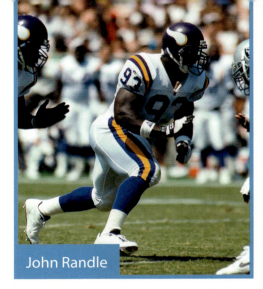

John Randle

Games: 219
Tackles: 556
Sacks: 137.5
Forced fumbles: 29
Fumble recoveries: 11
Touchdowns: 1
Awards: Seven Pro Bowls, six First Team All-Pro

ED REED S

Baltimore Ravens (2002–12),
Houston Texans (2013), New York
Jets (2013)

Ed Reed was the beating heart of Baltimore's defense for 11 seasons. He was a rangy ball hawk in the secondary who was as intelligent as he was athletic. Many of his interceptions resulted from knowledge he gained during film study of opposing quarterbacks. His 64 career interceptions rank seventh of all time. Once the ball was in his hands, Reed was even more dangerous. He made the two longest interception returns in NFL history, 107 and 106 yards, both for touchdowns.

Games: 174
Interceptions: 64
Tackles: 646
Sacks: 6
Touchdowns: 13
Awards: NFL Defensive Player of the Year (2004), nine Pro Bowls, five First Team All-Pro

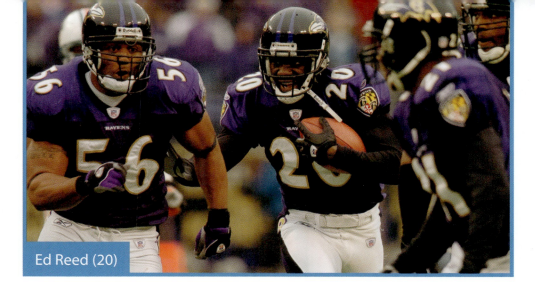

Ed Reed (20)

JERRY RICE WR

San Francisco 49ers (1985–2000),
Oakland Raiders (2001–04),
Seattle Seahawks (2004)

Many people say that Jerry Rice is the greatest receiver in NFL history. As the career leader in nearly every receiving category, Rice dominated the game. Teaming first with Joe Montana and then Steve Young, he led the NFL in receiving yards and touchdowns six times each. He was known for his taxing workouts that kept him in top physical condition. He excelled at running precise routes and blocking for his teammates. His 303 games played are the most of any wide receiver.

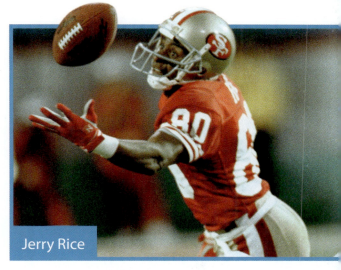

Jerry Rice

Games: 303
Receptions: 1,549
Receiving yards: 22,895
Receiving touchdowns: 197
Awards: NFL MVP (1987), Super Bowl MVP (1988), NFL Offensive Player of the Year (1987, 1993), 13 Pro Bowls, ten First Team All-Pro

BARRY SANDERS RB
Detroit Lions (1989–98)

Barry Sanders didn't have a nickname or a touchdown dance. In fact, he was known for handing the ball to the nearest official after every score. But no running back was more exciting in the open field than Sanders. His spins and quick moves left would-be tacklers grasping at air. Sanders led the NFL in rushing four times. He was second in career rushing yards, fewer than 1,500 behind Walter Payton, when he retired at age 30.

Barry Sanders

Games: 153
Rushing yards: 15,269
Rushing touchdowns: 99
Receptions: 352
Receiving yards: 2,921
Receiving touchdowns: 10
Awards: NFL MVP (1997), NFL Offensive Player of the Year (1994, 1997), NFL Offensive Rookie of the Year (1989), ten Pro Bowls, six First Team All-Pro

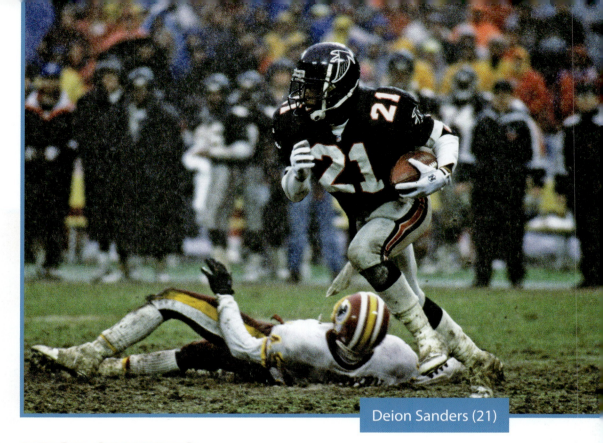

DEION SANDERS CB-KR

Atlanta Falcons (1989–93), San Francisco 49ers (1994), Dallas Cowboys (1995–99), Washington Redskins (2000), Baltimore Ravens (2004–05)

Deion Sanders was one of the most dynamic players and personalities the NFL has ever seen. Sanders was a dominant shutdown cornerback and one of the league's greatest punt returners. He also was an elite showman, high-stepping into the end zone and promoting himself in media interviews. Sanders won a Super Bowl in his only season with the 49ers, then jumped to the rival Cowboys and won it again the next year. He also played Major League Baseball for parts of nine seasons.

Games: 188
Interceptions: 53
Tackles: 512
Touchdowns: 22
Awards: NFL Defensive Player of the Year (1994), eight Pro Bowls, six First Team All-Pro

JUNIOR SEAU LB

San Diego Chargers (1990–2002), Miami Dolphins (2003–05), New England Patriots (2006–09)

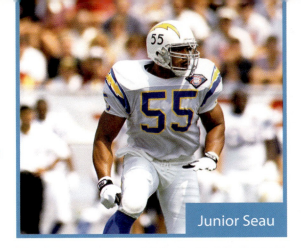

Junior Seau

Junior Seau was the heart and soul of the Chargers for more than a decade. He helped them to the Super Bowl after the 1994 season, when he led the NFL in solo tackles. He played with passion and fire that was contagious among his teammates, who looked to him as the leader.

Games: 268
Tackles: 1,847
Sacks: 56.5
Interceptions: 18
Fumble recoveries: 18
Touchdowns: 1
Awards: 12 Pro Bowls, six First Team All-Pro

BRUCE SMITH DE

Buffalo Bills (1985–99), Washington Redskins (2000–03)

A key cog in Buffalo's four-straight AFC champion teams, Bruce Smith was one of the most feared pass rushers in NFL history. Though he holds the NFL record for career sacks, he never led the league in a single season, which is evidence of his consistency and longevity. Smith posted double-digit sack totals in 13 seasons and led the NFL in forced fumbles twice.

Games: 279
Tackles: 1,224
Sacks: 200
Forced fumbles: 43
Fumble recoveries: 15
Touchdowns: 1
Awards: NFL Defensive Player of the Year (1990, 1996), 11 Pro Bowls, eight First Team All-Pro

Bruce Smith

EMMITT SMITH RB

Dallas Cowboys (1990–2002),
Arizona Cardinals (2003–04)

Emmitt Smith is the NFL's all-time rushing leader. Smith and his teammates Troy Aikman and Michael Irvin were known as the "Triplets." They carried the Cowboys to six division titles and three Super Bowl victories in the 1990s. Smith was a patient runner. He waited for his offensive line to execute their blocks before he blasted through the hole and gashed the opposing defense. He was especially productive near the end zone. His 164 rushing touchdowns are 19 more than any other NFL running back.

Emmitt Smith

Games: 226
Rushing yards: 18,355
Rushing touchdowns: 164
Receptions: 515
Receiving yards: 3,224
Receiving touchdowns: 11
Awards: NFL MVP (1993), NFL Offensive Rookie of the Year (1990), Super Bowl MVP (1993), eight Pro Bowls, four First Team All-Pro

Lawrence Taylor

LAWRENCE TAYLOR LB
New York Giants (1981–93)

Lawrence Taylor wasted no time showing the NFL that his mix of speed and strength was going to be hard to stop. He was the first rookie to win the NFL Defensive Player of the Year Award. He led the Giants to their first playoff berth of the Super Bowl era. He went on to star for two Super Bowl–winning teams in New York. Taylor also revolutionized the role of the pass-rushing linebacker. He posted 20.5 sacks in 1986 when he was named the NFL MVP. Taylor also led the Giants to their first Super Bowl.

Games: 184
Sacks: 132.5
Interceptions: 9
Fumble recoveries: 11
Touchdowns: 2
Awards: NFL MVP (1986), NFL Defensive Player of the Year (1981–82, 1986), NFL Defensive Rookie of the Year (1981), ten Pro Bowls, eight First Team All-Pro

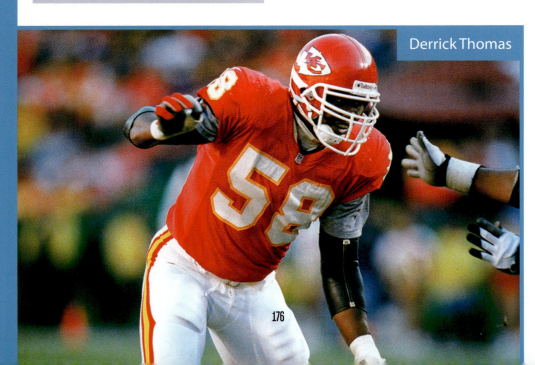

Derrick Thomas

176

DERRICK THOMAS LB

Kansas City Chiefs (1989–99)

An electric pass-rusher, Derrick Thomas used his speed from the edge to blow past opposing tackles and terrorize quarterbacks. In his second season, he set the NFL single-game sack record with seven against the Seahawks. Thomas led the league with a career-best 20 sacks that season. He also was an expert at forcing fumbles as he took the quarterback down.

Games: 169
Tackles: 641
Sacks: 126.5
Forced fumbles: 41
Fumble recoveries: 19
Touchdowns: 4
Awards: NFL Defensive Rookie of the Year (1989), nine Pro Bowls, two First Team All-Pro

JOE THOMAS T

Cleveland Browns (2007–17)

Joe Thomas

Joe Thomas was the No. 3 pick in the 2007 draft. He was a constant presence at left tackle for 11 seasons in Cleveland. He didn't miss a game in his first ten seasons. In fact, he didn't even miss a *play*. Thomas played 10,363 consecutive snaps. That's the most since the NFL started tracking snap counts in 1999. He was named to the Pro Bowl in each of his first ten seasons. He retired after suffering a torn tricep in a 2017 game.

Games: 167
Fumble recoveries: 10
Awards: Ten Pro Bowls, six First Team All-Pro

LaDainian
Tomlinson (21)

LaDAINIAN TOMLINSON RB

San Diego Chargers (2001–09), New York Jets (2010–11)

LaDainian Tomlinson was an amazing running back. He set NFL records with 28 rushing touchdowns and 31 combined touchdowns in 2006. He also led the league with a career-high 1,815 rushing yards that season, the first of two straight rushing titles for Tomlinson. He also threw seven career touchdown passes on option plays.

Games: 170
Rushing yards: 13,684
Rushing touchdowns: 145
Receptions: 624
Receiving yards: 4,772
Receiving touchdowns: 17
Awards: NFL MVP (2006), NFL Offensive Player of the Year (2006), five Pro Bowls, three First Team All-Pro

JOHNNY UNITAS QB

Baltimore Colts (1956–72),
San Diego Chargers (1973)

People view Johnny Unitas as the first modern quarterback. His Colts teams liked to pass in an era when the running game was still dominant in the league. Unitas led the league in passing yards and touchdown passes four times each. He was the first quarterback to throw for 30 touchdowns in a season. Unitas was also the first to reach 40,000 career passing yards. He threw a touchdown pass in 47 straight games, a record that stood for 52 years.

Games: 211
Passing yards: 40,239
Passing touchdowns: 290
Rushing yards: 450
Rushing touchdowns: 13
Awards: NFL MVP (1959, 1964, 1967), ten Pro Bowls, five First Team All-Pro

Johnny Unitas

GENE UPSHAW G
Oakland Raiders (1967–81)

Gene Upshaw started every game for the Raiders for 14 seasons. He holds the unique record of being the only player to participate in the Super Bowl for the same team in three different decades. He worked on an offensive line that anchored two NFL championship teams. He later served 25 years as the executive director of the NFL Players Association.

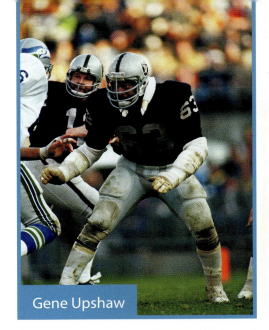
Gene Upshaw

Games: 217
Fumble recoveries: 5
Awards: Seven Pro Bowls, five First Team All-Pro

BRIAN URLACHER LB
Chicago Bears (2000–12)

Brian Urlacher was a versatile athlete. He played defensive back, wide receiver, and kick returner in college. Urlacher became the latest in a long line of talented Bears linebackers. He was a big part of Chicago's opportunistic defenses, which thrived on creating turnovers and scoring game-changing touchdowns. One year after winning the NFL Defensive Player of the Year Award, Urlacher led the Bears to the NFC title. He retired as the leading tackler in Bears history.

Games: 182
Tackles: 1,361
Sacks: 41.5
Interceptions: 22
Fumble recoveries: 15
Touchdowns: 5
Awards: NFL Defensive Rookie of the Year (2000), NFL Defensive Player of the Year (2005), eight Pro Bowls, four First-Team All-Pro

Brian Urlacher

Mike Webster

MIKE WEBSTER c

Pittsburgh Steelers (1974–88),
Kansas City Chiefs (1989–90)

Mike Webster was a fifth-round draft pick in 1974. He became an understudy to veteran Ray Mansfield for two seasons. Webster then served as the Steelers' starting center for 13 seasons. He was also the team's offensive captain for nine years. A durable force on the offensive line, Webster started every game for ten straight seasons. When he retired, Webster had played more seasons and games than any player in Steelers history.

Games: 245
Fumble recoveries: 6
Awards: Nine Pro Bowls, five First Team All-Pro

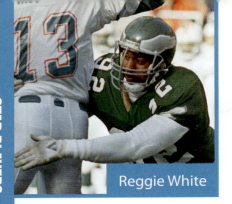

Reggie White

REGGIE WHITE DE

Philadelphia Eagles (1985–92), Green Bay Packers (1993–98), Carolina Panthers (2000)

Reggie White was an unstoppable force as a pass rusher. He averaged more than one sack per game in his eight years with the Eagles. That included his amazing 1987 season, when he got 21 sacks in just 12 games. In 1993 he signed as a free agent with the Packers. White is credited with jump-starting the Packers 1990s teams that included two Super Bowl appearances. He had three sacks in Green Bay's victory over New England in the Super Bowl after the 1996 season.

Games: 232
Tackles: 1,111
Sacks: 198
Forced fumbles: 33
Fumble recoveries: 20
Touchdowns: 2
Awards: NFL Defensive Player of the Year (1987–1988), 13 Pro Bowls, eight First Team All-Pro

CHARLES WOODSON DB

Oakland Raiders (1998–2005, 2013–15), Green Bay Packers (2006–12)

Charles Woodson wasn't afraid to get involved in stopping the run or blitzing the quarterback. His 65 career interceptions are fifth in NFL history. Woodson became the first player to return at least one interception for a touchdown in six consecutive seasons. Woodson's 13 defensive touchdowns are tied for the most in NFL history.

Games: 254
Interceptions: 65
Tackles: 1,220
Sacks: 20
Touchdowns: 13
Awards: NFL Defensive Rookie of the Year (1998), NFL Defensive Player of the Year (2009), nine Pro Bowls, four First Team All-Pro

Charles Woodson

ROD WOODSON DB

Pittsburgh Steelers (1987–96), San Francisco 49ers (1997), Baltimore Ravens (1998–01), Oakland Raiders (2002–03)

Rod Woodson was a dynamic athlete. He earned All-Pro honors at cornerback, safety, and kick returner. Only two players intercepted more passes than Woodson, and he's one of three players with 13 career defensive touchdowns. He made seven Pro Bowl appearances during his time with the Steelers.

Rod Woodson

Later in his career, Woodson was a veteran leader in Baltimore. He helped the Ravens win a Super Bowl while their defense set NFL records for fewest points and rushing yards allowed in 2000.

Games: 238
Interceptions: 71
Tackles: 1,158
Sacks: 13.5
Touchdowns: 17
Awards: NFL Defensive Player of the Year (1993), 11 Pro Bowls, six First Team All-Pro

HONORABLE MENTIONS

Eric Allen (CB): Philadelphia Eagles (1988–94), New Orleans Saints (1995–97), Oakland Raiders (1998–2001)

Marcus Allen (RB): Los Angeles Raiders (1982–92), Kansas City Chiefs (1993–97)

Chuck Bednarik (C-LB): Philadelphia Eagles (1949–62)

Bobby Bell (LB-DE): Kansas City Chiefs (1963–74)

Raymond Berry (WR): Baltimore Colts (1955–67)

Tim Brown (WR): Los Angeles Raiders (1988–94), Oakland Raiders (1995–2003), Tampa Bay Buccaneers (2004)

Earl Campbell (RB): Houston Oilers (1978–84), New Orleans Saints (1984–85)

Cris Carter (WR): Philadelphia Eagles (1987–89), Minnesota Vikings (1990–2001), Miami Dolphins (2002)

Willie Davis (DL): Cleveland Browns (1958–59), Green Bay Packers (1960–69)

Eric Dickerson (RB): Los Angeles Rams (1983–87), Indianapolis Colts (1987–91), Los Angeles Raiders (1992), Atlanta Falcons (1993)

Carl Eller (DE): Minnesota Vikings (1964–78), Seattle Seahawks (1979)

John Elway (QB): Denver Broncos (1983–98)

Marshall Faulk (RB): Indianapolis Colts (1994–98), St. Louis Rams (1999–2005)

Brett Favre (QB): Atlanta Falcons (1991), Green Bay Packers (1992–2007), New York Jets (2008), Minnesota Vikings (2009–10)

Antonio Gates (TE): San Diego Chargers (2003–16), Los Angeles Chargers (2017–18)

Kevin Greene (LB-DE): Los Angeles Rams (1985–92), Pittsburgh Steelers (1993–95), Carolina Panthers (1996, 1998–99), San Francisco 49ers (1997)

Charles Haley (DE-LB): San Francisco 49ers (1986–91, 1999), Dallas Cowboys (1992–96)

Jack Ham (LB): Pittsburgh Steelers (1971–82)

Marvin Harrison (WR): Indianapolis Colts (1996–2008)

Rodney Harrison (DB): San Diego Chargers (1994–2002), New England Patriots (2003–08)

Mike Haynes (CB): New England Patriots (1976–82), Los Angeles Raiders (1983–89)

Ken Houston (DB): Houston Oilers (1967–72), Washington Redskins (1973–80)

Sam Huff (LB): New York Giants (1956–63), Washington Redskins (1964–69)

Michael Irvin (WR): Dallas Cowboys (1988–99)

Rickey Jackson (LB-DE): New Orleans Saints (1981–93), San Francisco 49ers (1994–95)

Walter Jones (T): Seattle Seahawks (1997–2008)

Jerry Kramer (G): Green Bay Packers (1958–69)

Willie Lanier (LB): Kansas City Chiefs (1967–77)

Larry Little (G): San Diego Chargers (1967–68), Miami Dolphins (1969–80)

Dan Marino (QB): Miami Dolphins (1983–99)

Randall McDaniel (G): Minnesota Vikings (1988–99), Tampa Bay Buccaneers (2000–01)

Warren Moon (QB): Houston Oilers (1984–93), Minnesota Vikings (1994–96), Seattle Seahawks (1997–98), Kansas City Chiefs (1999–2000)

Ray Nitschke (LB): Green Bay Packers (1958–72)

Merlin Olsen (DT): Los Angeles Rams (1962–76)

Troy Polamalu (S): Pittsburgh Steelers (2003–14)

Willie Roaf (T): New Orleans Saints (1993–2001), Kansas City Chiefs (2002–05)

Aaron Rodgers (QB): Green Bay Packers (2005–)

Gale Sayers (RB): Chicago Bears (1965–71)

Lee Roy Selmon (DE): Tampa Bay Buccaneers (1976–84)

Art Shell (T): Oakland Raiders (1968–81), Los Angeles Raiders (1982)

Will Shields (G): Kansas City Chiefs (1993–2006)

Bubba Smith (DE): Baltimore Colts (1967–71), Oakland Raiders (1973–74), Houston Oilers (1975–76)

Bart Starr (QB): Green Bay Packers (1956–71)

Roger Staubach (QB): Dallas Cowboys (1969–79)

Michael Strahan (DE): New York Giants (1993–2007)

Emmitt Thomas (DB): Kansas City Chiefs (1966–77)

J. J. Watt (DE): Houston Texans (2011–20), Arizona Cardinals (2021–)

Randy White (DT): Dallas Cowboys (1975–88)

Aeneas Williams (DB): Phoenix Cardinals (1991–93), Arizona Cardinals (1994–2000), St. Louis Rams (2001–04)

Steve Young (QB): Tampa Bay Buccaneers (1985–86), San Francisco 49ers (1987–99)

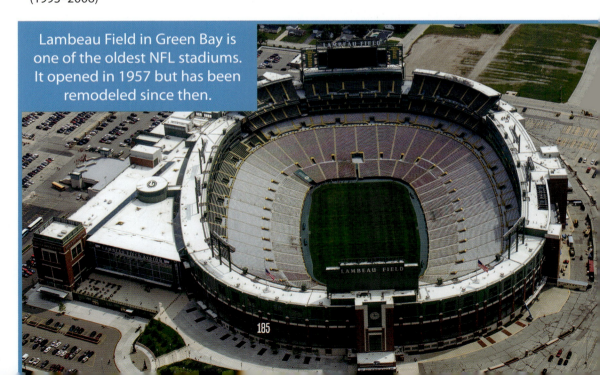

Lambeau Field in Green Bay is one of the oldest NFL stadiums. It opened in 1957 but has been remodeled since then.

185

NFL ALL-TIME LEADERS (THROUGH 2020)

PASSING LEADERS

ATTEMPTS
1. Tom Brady* _____ 10,598
2. Drew Brees* _____ 10,551
3. Brett Favre _____ 10,169
4. Peyton Manning _____ 9,380
5. Dan Marino _____ 8,358

COMPLETIONS
1. Drew Brees* _____ 7,142
2. Tom Brady* _____ 6,778
3. Brett Favre _____ 6,300
4. Peyton Manning _____ 6,125
5. Philip Rivers* _____ 5,277

PASSING YARDS
1. Drew Brees* _____ 80,358
2. Tom Brady* _____ 79,204
3. Peyton Manning _____ 71,940
4. Brett Favre _____ 71,838
5. Philip Rivers* _____ 63,440

TOUCHDOWN PASSES
1. Tom Brady* _____ 581
2. Drew Brees* _____ 571
3. Peyton Manning _____ 539
4. Brett Favre _____ 508
5. Philip Rivers* _____ 421

PASSES INTERCEPTED
1. Brett Favre _____ 336
2. George Blanda _____ 277
3. John Hadl _____ 268
4. Vinny Testaverde _____ 267
5. Fran Tarkenton _____ 266

COMPLETION PERCENTAGE
(MINIMUM 1,500 ATTEMPTS)
1. Deshaun Watson* _____ 67.8
2. Drew Brees* _____ 67.7
3. Kirk Cousins* _____ 67.0
4. Teddy Bridgewater* _____ 66.5
5. Patrick Mahomes* _____ 66.0
5. Chad Pennington _____ 66.0
5. Dak Prescott* _____ 66.0

RUSHING LEADERS

RUSHES
1. Emmitt Smith _____ 4,409
2. Walter Payton _____ 3,838
3. Frank Gore* _____ 3,735
4. Curtis Martin _____ 3,518
5. Jerome Bettis _____ 3,479

RUSHING YARDS
1. Emmitt Smith _____ 18,355
2. Walter Payton _____ 16,726
3. Frank Gore* _____ 16,000
4. Barry Sanders _____ 15,269
5. Adrian Peterson* _____ 14,820

RUSHING TOUCHDOWNS
1. Emmitt Smith _____ 164
2. LaDainian Tomlinson _____ 145
3. Marcus Allen _____ 123
4. Adrian Peterson* _____ 118
5. Walter Payton _____ 110

RECEPTIONS BY AN RB
1. Larry Centers _____ 827
2. Marshall Faulk _____ 767
3. LaDainian Tomlinson _____ 624
4. Keith Byars _____ 610
5. Marcus Allen _____ 587

RECEIVING YARDS BY AN RB
1. Marshall Faulk _____ 6,875
2. Larry Centers _____ 6,797
3. Ronnie Harmon _____ 6,076
4. Keith Byars _____ 5,661
5. Eric Metcalf _____ 5,572

TOUCHDOWN RECEPTIONS BY AN RB
1. Marshall Faulk _____ 36
2. Darren Sproles _____ 32
3. Keith Byars _____ 31
4. Larry Centers _____ 28
5. Ronnie Harmon _____ 24

RECEIVING LEADERS

RECEPTIONS
1. Jerry Rice _____ 1,549
2. Larry Fitzgerald* _____ 1,432
3. Tony Gonzalez _____ 1,325
4. Jason Witten* _____ 1,228
5. Marvin Harrison _____ 1,102

RECEIVING YARDS
1. Jerry Rice _____ 22,895
2. Larry Fitzgerald* _____ 17,492
3. Terrell Owens _____ 15,934
4. Randy Moss _____ 15,292
5. Isaac Bruce _____ 15,208

TOUCHDOWN RECEPTIONS
1. Jerry Rice _____ 197
2. Randy Moss _____ 156
3. Terrell Owens _____ 153
4. Cris Carter _____ 130
5. Marvin Harrison _____ 128

DEFENSIVE LEADERS (SOLO)

TACKLES
1. Ray Lewis _____ 1,568
2. London Fletcher _____ 1,384
3. Derrick Brooks _____ 1,300
4. Donnie Edwards _____ 1,135
5. Zach Thomas _____ 1,107

SACKS (SINCE 1982)
1. Bruce Smith _____ 200
2. Reggie White _____ 198
3. Kevin Greene _____ 160
4. Julius Peppers _____ 159.5
5. Chris Doleman _____ 150.5

INTERCEPTIONS
1. Paul Krause _____ 81
2. Emlen Tunnell _____ 79
3. Rod Woodson _____ 71
4. Dick Lane _____ 68
5. Ken Riley _____ 65
5. Charles Woodson _____ 65

FORCED FUMBLES
1. Robert Mathis _____ 54
2. Julius Peppers _____ 52
3. John Abraham _____ 47
3. Dwight Freeney _____ 47
4. Jason Taylor _____ 46

FUMBLE RECOVERIES
1. Rod Woodson _____ 32
2. Jim Marshall _____ 30
3. Rickey Jackson _____ 29
3. Jason Taylor _____ 29
4. Kermit Alexander _____ 28

KICKING LEADERS

POINTS
1. Adam Vinatieri _____ 2,673
2. Morten Andersen _____ 2,544
3. Gary Anderson _____ 2,434
4. Jason Hanson _____ 2,150
5. John Carney _____ 2,062

FIELD GOALS MADE
1. Adam Vinatieri _____ 599
2. Morten Andersen _____ 565
3. Gary Anderson _____ 538
4. Jason Hanson _____ 495
5. John Carney _____ 478

FIELD GOAL PERCENTAGE
1. Justin Tucker* _____ 90.7
2. Harrison Butker* _____ 90.3
3. Josh Lambo* _____ 88.9
4. Chris Boswell* _____ 88.0
5. Wil Lutz* _____ 86.6

EXTRA POINTS MADE
1. George Blanda _____ 943
2. Adam Vinatieri _____ 874
3. Morten Andersen _____ 849
4. Gary Anderson _____ 820
5. Lou Groza _____ 810

PUNTING LEADERS

PUNTS
1. Jeff Feagles _____ 1,713
2. Shane Lechler _____ 1,444
3. Sean Landetta _____ 1,401
4. Andy Lee* _____ 1,348
5. Brad Maynard _____ 1,339

PUNTING YARDS
1. Jeff Feagles _____ 71,211
2. Shane Lechler _____ 68,676
3. Andy Lee* _____ 62,747
4. Sean Landeta _____ 60,707
5. Brad Maynard _____ 56,021

AVERAGE PUNT
1. Shane Lechler _____ 47.6
2. Johnny Hekker* _____ 46.9
3. Tress Way* _____ 46.8
4. Marquette King _____ 46.7
4. Brandon Fields _____ 46.7

* Indicates player is active as of 2020

GLOSSARY

commissioner
A person appointed to regulate a particular sport.

controversy
Something that gives rise to public disagreement.

debut
A person or team's first appearance in a specific role.

dynasty
An extended period of excellence or success for a team.

franchise
A professional sports team that is part of a league.

free agent
A player whose rights are not owned by any team.

iconic
Having the characteristics of someone or something that is very famous or popular.

integrate
To incorporate people belonging to different groups (such as races) into areas of society from which they have been excluded.

interception
A pass intended for an offensive player that is caught by a defensive player.

merger
The act of combining two or more organizations to create a single larger one.

overtime
Extra time played at the end of regulation time.

rookie
An athlete in his or her first full season in a sport.

strike
A workers' protest that involves refusing to work until requests are met.

turnover
When one team loses possession of the ball to the other team by a fumble or interception.

upset
To unexpectedly beat a team or player who was heavily favored to win.

veteran
A player who has played many years in the league.

TO LEARN MORE

FURTHER READINGS

Harris, Duchess, and Cynthia Kennedy Henzel. *Politics and Protest in Sports*. Abdo, 2019.

Martin, Brett S. *STEM in Football*. Abdo, 2018.

Wilner, Barry. *Great Football Debates*. Abdo, 2019.

ONLINE RESOURCES

To learn more about the NFL, please visit **abdobooklinks.com** or scan this QR code. These links are routinely monitored and updated to provide the most current information available.

INDEX

PHOTO CREDITS

Previously titled The NFL Encyclopedia for Kids

First Edition
First Printing, 2021

THIS BOOK CONTAINS
RECYCLED MATERIALS

Editor: Alyssa Sorenson
Series Designer: Colleen McLaren
Cover Designer: Jake Slavik

ISBN: 978-1-952455-09-4 (paperback)

Library of Congress Control Number: 2021917057

Distributed in paperback by North Star Editions, Inc.
2297 Waters Drive
Mendota Heights, MN 55120
www.northstareditions.com

Printed in the United States of America